Derelicts

for Steven Fennell —

I hope you enjoy this!

Jack C. Haeger

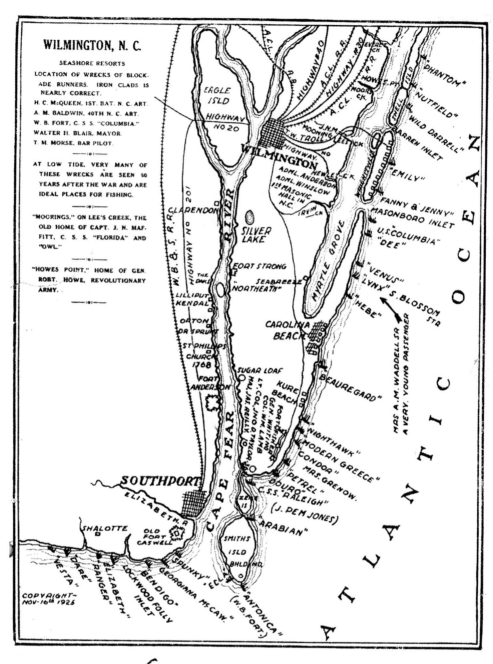

The 1925 Robert N. Sweet map of the Cape Fear, showing Civil War-era shipwrecks and other points of interest.

Derelicts

An account of ships lost at sea in general commerce and a brief history of blockade runners stranded along the North Carolina coast
1861 - 1865

by
James Sprunt
author of
Chronicles of the Cape Fear River: 1660 - 1916

edited by
Jack E. Fryar, Jr.

Originally published in 1920 by
The Lord Baltimore Press
BALTIMORE, MD., U. S. A.

This new, illustrated edition published by

Dram Tree
Books
A JEF Publications Company

First Printing 1922
This illustrated edition 2006

Published in the United States of America by Dram Tree Books,
a JEF Publications company.

Publisher's Cataloging-in-Publication Data
(Provided by DRT Press)

Sprunt, James, 1846-1924.
   Derelicts: an account of ships lost at sea in general commerce traffic and a brief history of blockade runners stranded along the North Carolina coast 1861-1865 / by James Sprunt ; edited by Jack E. Fryar, Jr.

   p. cm
   Includes bibliographical references and index.
   "New, illustrated edition"
   ISBN 0-9723240-9-7

1. Derelicts. 2. United States--History--Civil War, 1861 - 1865--Blockades 3. North Carolina--History--Civil War, 1861 - 1865. 4. Wilmington (N.C.)--History--Civil War, 1861 - 1865. I. Fryar, Jack E. II. Title.

E600 .S77 2006
973.757

10 9 8 7 6 5 4 3 2 1
Dram Tree Books
549 Eagle Lane
Southport, N.C. 28461
(910) 538-4076
dramtreebooks@ec.rr.com

*Discounts available
for educators.
Call or e-mail for terms.*

Contents

List of Illustrations

Foreword

About twenty-five years ago I wrote for the *Southport Leader* a series of stories of the Cape Fear blockade from my personal experiences as a participant in the blockade runners *Advance, Eugenie, North Heath, Lilian, Susan Beirne*, and finally in the *Alonzo*, which greatly interested the Cape Fear pilots who had taken part with me in this hazardous service and were found entertaining by some other readers. Later, in the year 1901, I contributed at the request of Chief Justice Walter Clark for his admirable *North Carolina Regimental Histories* an account of my personal adventures and observations in the *North Heath, Lilian*, and *Susan Beirne*, in the capacity of purser, or paymaster, at the age of seventeen and a half years, and as prisoner of war on the *Keystone State* and the *Glaucus*, Federal cruisers, and later prisoner of war in Fort Macon and in Fortress Monroe.

Again, in 1914, I wrote in the *Cape Fear Chronicles* at some length on this interesting phase of Cape Fear history, in the form largely of personal reminiscences, which have been most generously commented.

James Sprunt
Wilmington, N.C.
1920

"Some night to the lee of the land I shall steal,
(Heigh-ho to be home from the sea!)
No pilot but Death at the rudderless wheel,
(None knoweth the harbor as he!)
To lie where the slow tide creeps hither and fro
And the shifting sand laps me around, for I know
That my gallant old crew are in Port long ago—
Forever at peace with the sea!"

The Song of the Derelict.
Lieutenant-Colonel John McCrae.

Marine Wanderers

Years before the beginning of the Great War I took passage from New York for Liverpool in one of the most beautiful examples of marine architecture of that era. When we were about a thousand miles from Queenstown, our port of call, we sighted a vessel in distress, dismasted and water-logged, crowded as we thought with passengers. Our course was changed to carry us nearer the vessel, when we perceived that what we thought were human beings on deck were the bare ribs of a barque from St. John's, New Brunswick, loaded with timber, and that the dynamic force of the sea had broken away the vessel's bulwarks, leaving the frame standing, which resembled a crowd of men. A derelict abandoned upon the wide ocean, staggering like a drunken man on the heaving bosom of the sea, a menace to every vessel upon the great highway of commerce, this mass of unwieldy timber was a greater danger in the darkness than any other peril of the ocean. To my surprise and indignation our captain turned away from the wreck without attempting its destruction by dynamite as he was in duty bound to compass. We were one of the famous flyers of that day and could not afford, he said, to reduce our record of speed by any delay.

Three months after this incident I was returning homeward on the same steamer, and when we were at least 2,000 miles from Queenstown I sighted, through a powerful binocular, a wreck ahead, and as we approached nearer I said to the first officer, "That is the derelict we passed three months ago." He laughed at the idea of such a thing. "Why," said he, "she is thousands of miles away in another current if she is still afloat." But my observation was correct. We ran close to the same vessel that we had seen three months before. What destruction of life and property she had wrought mean-time, no one could tell, and we again disgraced the service by leaving her untouched.

The meaning of a derelict in law is a thing voluntarily abandoned or willfully cast away by its proper owner; especially a ship abandoned at sea.

Mr. William Allingham, author of *A Manual of Marine Meteorology*, whom I quote at length, says in *Chambers's Edinburgh Journal*, February, 1912:

"Every storm that travels over the waters which divide, yet unite, the New World and the Old, leaves in its wake some sailing ship abandoned by her crew. As a rule these dreaded derelicts are of wooden build and laden with cargoes of lumber. Often they have carried costly cargoes under every sky with credit to themselves and profit to their owners, but the increasing infirmities of age have caused them to engage in the lowliest forms of ocean-carrying. Under the adverse influence of a careering cyclone these gallant craft meet their fate. The savage sea opens wide their straining seams; the pumps, clatter as they may, are quite unable to cope with the ingress of sea water; and the disheartened crews seek safety in a passing ship at the first opportunity. Thus it happens that many a lumber-laden sailing ship drifts deviously at the will of wind and current, a menace to safe navigation, until her hull is driven into fragments by the combined forces of Aeolus and Neptune, or reaches land after a solitary drift of many weary leagues of sea.

"Quite naturally, the North Atlantic holds the record for drifting derelicts, inasmuch as it is the great ocean highway of the nations. During the five years 1887 to 1891 not fewer than 957 derelict ships were reported to the Hydrographer at Washington, then Capt. (now Admiral) Richardson Clover, U. S. Navy, as in evidence between the fifty-second meridian of west longitude and the east coast of North America. Of this large number 332 were identified by name, and the remainder were either capsized or battered out of recognition. On an average there were about twenty derelicts drifting in the North Atlantic at any instant, and the life of each was one month. The

Washington Hydrographic Office receives reports from shipmasters under every flag setting forth the appearance and the geographical position of every derelict sighted during the passage across, and this information is published in the weekly Hydrographic Bulletins and the monthly Pilot Charts, which are freely distributed among navigators visiting American ports by the branch offices of that department of the United States Navy. The British Board of Trade also furnishes shipmasters in United Kingdom ports with similar printed information, and the British Meteorological Office has followed suit by graphic representation on their monthly Pilot Charts of the North Atlantic.

"Many derelicts disappear within a few days of abandonment, but some drift several thousand miles before the end comes. A vessel left to her fate near New York, for example, may drift southward with the Labrador current until not far from Cape Hatteras. Thence she finds a way into the relatively warm waters of the Gulf Stream, and may eventually drift ashore on the west coast of Europe. Should the derelict happen to get into the Sargasso Sea, an area in mid-Atlantic of light winds and variable currents, made memorable by the pen of Julius Chambers, she will probably travel in a circle for a long series of days.

"The schooner *W. L. White*, abandoned during the blizzard of March, 1888, just eastward of the Delaware Capes, made tracks for the Banks of Newfoundland; there she remained for many days, right on the route of palatial passenger liners; then she got another slant to the northeast, and eventually drove ashore at Haskeir Island, one of the Hebrides, after traversing 6,800 miles in 310 days. Her timber cargo was salved by the islanders in fairly good condition.

"Metal ships are seldom left derelict; but there are not wanting remarkable verified drifts even of this class. In October, 1876, the British iron barque *Ada Iredale* was abandoned, with her coal cargo burning fiercely, when 2,000 miles east of the Marquesas Islands, South Pacific. She moved slowly westward with the south equatorial current, traveled 2,500 miles in 241 days, and was then picked up by a French warship, which towed her to Tahiti. After the fire had died out the hull was repaired; she was fitted with new masts and rigging, and has ever since been known as the *Annie Johnson* of San Francisco, Cal. On her being boarded some time ago, she was still doing well and quite a handsome vessel. In April, 1882, the *Falls of Afton* was precipitately abandoned while on the way from Glasgow to Calcutta with a valuable cargo. A few days later she was picked up by a French vessel and taken to Madeira. Since that time she has had many

The iron barque **Ada Iredale** *before she was abandoned off the Marquesas in 1876.*

successful voyages; but the master at the time of her abandonment suffered severely under the finding of a court of inquiry.

"Ships which have been abandoned more than once in their career are not unknown. In November, 1888, the iron ship *Duncow* stranded close to Dunkirk Harbor during heavy weather. The crew sought safety on shore, and the ship afterwards floated. Belgian fishermen boarded the derelict, obtained the services of a tug, and took her to Terneuzen, thus assuring for themselves salvage payment, which could not have been legally claimed had she reached a French port. In 1897 this vessel, while carrying timber from Puget Sound to Australia, went ashore not far from her destination. She again floated off after abandonment; and once again a tugboat earned salvage by bringing the derelict into port uninjured.

"Derelict ships add to the difficulties of trans-Atlantic navigation; hence the demand of the shipping industry for specially constructed derelict destroyers, such as the American *Seneca*, to patrol the Atlantic, experience having shown that a derelict is not nearly so impossible to locate as is sometimes alleged. The barque *Siddartha* was abandoned near the Azores in February, 1899. She drifted slowly to the northeast until within 400 miles of

Queenstown, and there she hovered over the liner tracks for several successive weeks. Moved by a joint appeal of the White Star and Cunard Companies, the British Admiralty sent out two warships in quest of the derelict, and she was soon anchored in Bantry Bay. This vessel, while derelict, was reported to the United States Hydrographic Office by more than sixty ships. In February, 1895, the barque *Birgitte* was abandoned on the western side of the Atlantic; and on the 1st of March she was sighted about 1,000 miles west of Cape Clear. Drifting slowly eastward, almost continuously on the routes followed by the large trans-Atlantic liners, this derelict was found by a tugboat and towed into Queenstown. Forty-three vessels had reported her to Washington during the interval. At nighttime and in thick weather such dangers may be passed quite close without any one's having an inkling of their proximity. About the same date, but more to the northeast, the Russian barque *Louise* was abandoned. She apparently went north as far as the Faroe Islands, under the influence of the Gulf Stream extension; thence proceeded eastward; and was picked up by two steam trawlers when sixteen miles from Aalesund, Norway, and thence towed into that port, after a drift of approximately 1,400 miles. The American schooner *Alma Cumming* was left to her fate in February, 1895, off Chesapeake Bay. After the end of May nothing was heard from her until March, 1896, when she was about 800 miles off the Cape Verde Islands. She was then totally dismasted, had evidently been unsuccessfully set on fire by some passing ship, and her deck was level with the sea surface. In August she was observed ashore on an island off the San Blas coast, Isthmus of Panama, with the natives busily engaged annexing all they could from the wreck. On the 1st of March, 1911, in 53 deg. N., 28 deg. W., the Russian steamer *Korea* was abandoned by her crew; and two days later, about a degree farther east, the steamer *Ionian* sustained considerable damage by collision with the derelict.

"Some of the reports of alleged derelict ships are as thrilling as a nautical novel. In May, 1823, the *Integrity* fell in with a derelict close to Jamaica, the decks and hull of which were showing a rich crop of barnacles. Her cabin was full of water, but a trunk was fished up which contained coins, rings, and watches. This salvage realized 3,000 pounds. In August, 1872, the schooner *Lancaster* sighted a dismasted derelict, the *Glenalvon*, on board of which several skeletons of men were discovered, but not a morsel of food. An open Bible, it is reported, lay face downward on the cabin table along-side a loaded revolver and a bottle containing a piece of paper on which was written: "Jesus, guide this to some helper! Merciful God, don't let us perish!" All the bodies were reverently committed to the deep, and the derelict left for whatever the future had in store for her.

"In 1882 the Nova Scotia barque *L. E. Cann* was towed into a United States port by a steamship which had found her adrift. Later on in dry dock, fifteen auger holes were located in her hull, below the water line. They had all been bored from the inside, and subsequent inquiry revealed the fact that her former captain had conspired with a resident of Vera Cruz to load the vessel with a bogus cargo, insure it heavily, scuttle her when in a suitable position at sea, and divide the insurance money. Unfortunately for these partners in crime, the barque did not lend herself to their nefarious operations nearly as well as was expected.

"In 1894 the Austrian barque *Vila*, carrying a cargo of bones, which were said to have been gathered from the battle fields of Egypt, was found derelict by a Norwegian steamer and towed into New York. Not a word has ever been heard as to the fate of this vessel's crew. Presumably they took to the boats for some reason, and disappeared without leaving a trace. About the same time the sailing vessel *C. E. Morrison* was fallen in with, a drifting derelict and set on fire. The crew of a destroyer first salved a bank-book, a sextant, fifty charts, and some pictures, all of which were eventually returned to their rightful owner, Captain Hawes, who had been compelled to leave his vessel without standing on the order of his going. In 1895 the derelict and burning barkantine *Celestina*, bound from Swansea to the Strait of Magellan, was boarded by a boat's crew of the barque *Annie Maud*. A written message was found on the cabin table stating that she had been abandoned in open boats. The fire having been partially subdued, sail was made on the prize, and volunteers navigated her to Rio Janeiro.

"The *Marie Celeste* is a mystery of the sea. This brig left America for Gibraltar; and nothing more was heard of her until she was sighted approaching the Strait in a suspicious manner, when she was found to be derelict. Her hull was sound, there was no sign of an accident aloft, and her boats were in their appointed places. Some remains of a meal on the cabin table were still fresh, and a watch was ticking unconcernedly; yet her captain and his wife and daughter, together with the crew, had disappeared forever.

"Nautical novelists have made moving pictures of drifting derelicts, and hoaxers have also utilized them. In 1893 some witty person closely copied parts of a soul-stirring yarn by Clark Russell, and the alleged modern experience was telegraphed round the world, appeared in the press, and was then decisively contradicted. It was asserted that the Norwegian ship *Elsa*

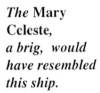

The **Mary Celeste,** *a brig, would have resembled this ship.*

Anderson arrived at Galveston with an English-built brig in tow, which had apparently been burned and sunk more than a half century previously. A submarine seismic disturbance was invented to account for the vessel's return to the surface. The hull was covered with strange seashells, and in the hold were chests containing many guineas bearing date 1800, several watches, and a stomacher of pearls! One of three skeletons was said to be that of a man over seven feet in height. This hoax was successful until it reached Galveston. Then the authorities denied that the story had the slighest foundation in fact. Six years later a similar hoax was perpetrated, which ought immediately to have been recognized as merely a variant of *The Frozen Pirate*, by the above-mentioned eminent nautical novelist. It was gravely asserted that the barque *Silicon*, on her way from the United States to Greenland, had picked up an old-fashioned derelict ship near the Greenland coast. When access to the hold was gained, the salvors, so ran the hoax, discovered that she was laden with furs in good condition; and her log book showed that she had been abandoned by her crew in 1848. Like the ship imagined by Clark Russell, she was said to have been fast in the ice in the far North. One of the most ridiculous derelict-ship hoaxes of the past century had quite a boom in 1896. A burning derelict, read an astonished world, had been passed between the Cape of Good Hope and Australia, with her lower holds full of coal and petroleum, and the between-decks portion crammed with the dead bodies of people who had met their fate by suffocation while on their way from Russia to Brazil. The burning cargo had generated gas which suffocated the emigrants; the bodies had swollen out of human shape, and subsequent explosions had torn many limb from limb! This tissue of falsehoods appeared in many of the world's daily papers without comment.

"*H.M.S. Resolute*, since broken up, was one of the most famous of derelicts. She was abandoned in 77 deg. 40 min. N., 101 deg. 20 min. W., drifted southward in the center of a solid sheet of ice, and was eventually

H.M.S. Resolute, *England's Arctic research ship, returning home after being found derelict in 1856.*

picked up by an American whaleship off Cape Mercy, in 65 deg. N. After having been refitted by the United States Government, she was presented to England with impressive ceremony. A desk of the President of the United States, in the White House, Washington, D. C., was made from the timbers of the *Resolute*, and sent by Her Majesty Queen Victoria in memory of that courtesy and loving-kindness of America to England. It is a substantial token of the good will existing between the two kindred peoples."

The gifted editor of our National Geographic Society's admirable magazine, Gilbert H. Grosvenor, in the September number, 1918, page 235, says on the subject of "Strange Stories of Derelicts," "How hard it is sometimes to send a ship to the bottom is strikingly shown by the experience of the *San Francisco* in destroying the derelict three-master *Drisko* a decade or so ago. That derelict was only 248 tons, but she was lumber laden. The officers of the *San Francisco* first tried to tow her to port, but found that impossible. Then they attached three 30-pound guncotton bombs to her keel and set them off, but still she floated. Five more bombs were set off; these broke her back and frames, but still she refused to go to the bottom. Then the *San Francisco* rammed her amidships and broke her in two, releasing the cargo; but even after that it took several shells to drive the afterpart of the staunch old schooner down into the jurisdiction of Davy Jones.

"Even in peace times ships are often reported missing, and appear to have been 'sunk without trace.' It is believed that most of such catastrophes are the result of collisions with derelicts. How many more such collisions there will be in the future may be imagined when it is stated that for two years the number of derelicts has greatly increased and the steps for their destruction have been much reduced.

"In peace times," continues Mr. Grosvenor, "there is no other menace to navigation as dangerous as the derelict, unless it be the submerged iceberg, such as sunk the *Titanic*. Refusing to stay in one location, yielding to no law of navigation, hiding most of her bulk beneath the waves, the lonely, desolate, moss-covered, weed-grown derelict, with deck or keel all but awash, comes out of the night or through the fog as an assassin out of a lonely alley, and woe to the sailor who has not detected her approach.

"Drifting hither and yon, now forced on by the wind of a stormy sea, now caught in a current and driven along, these rudderless, purposeless, wanderers cover many a weary mile, with only screaming sea birds to break the monotony of the roaring gale or the soft surge of a placid sea. Sighted frequently for weeks together, now and again they disappear, often reappearing suddenly hundreds of miles away. As many as a thousand have been reported in a single year in the North Atlantic. The majority of them frequent the Gulf Stream.

"Examining the records of the Hydrographic Office, one finds that in six years twenty-five derelicts were reported as having drifted at least a thousand miles each; eleven have 2,000 miles apiece to their credit, while three sailed 5,000 rudderless miles.

"The classic story of the wanderings of a derelict is that of the *Fannie E. Wolston.* Abandoned October 15, 1891, off Cape Hatteras, she traveled northward in the Gulf Stream. When off Norfolk, Va., she changed her course and headed across the broad Atlantic toward the shores of Africa. On June 13, 1892, she was sighted half way across. Then she headed southward for more than 300 miles; then shifted her course to the northeast for another 200 miles, retraced her track for several hundred miles, turned again and went in the opposite direction, like a shuttle in the loom instead of a ship upon the sea. Then she took another tack and headed west for nearly 400 miles; then shaped her course north for 300 miles, and then headed east again for 700 miles; so that in January she was almost in the same latitude and longitude that she had been in the previous June. In the following May she was a thousand miles away from where she had been in January, on the border of Cancer and midway between Florida and Africa. Again she headed toward America for 600 miles, and repeated her shuttle-in-the-loom performance. Then followed many long months of erratic zigzags and she was sighted for the last time 250 miles off Savannah, Ga. She had remained afloat and had out-generaled the waves for two years and a half, during which time she had sailed more than 7,000 aimless miles.

"In normal times," continues Mr. Grosvenor, "the Hydrographic Office of the Navy Department keeps careful check on the derelicts. Every ship that sights one of these menaces to navigation reports its location. The names of some of them remain visible, while others are susceptible of identification by their appearance. The Hydrographic Office gives each wreck and derelict a serial number and plots its position on a map. Each report is registered with an identification number. In this way, by a system of cross checking, it is possible to identify each derelict, to determine the direction of its drift, and usually to get it so well located that the Coast Guard cutters may run it down and sink it."

On January 16, 1919, I addressed an inquiry to the Coast and Geodetic Survey, Washington, on the subject of international protection of commerce in the destruction of derelicts, ice observation, etc., to which I received the following courteous reply from Commodore Bertholf, dated February 7, 1919:

"**1.** Your letter of January 16, addressed to the Coast Geodetic Survey, seeking information on the subject of an arrangement between our Federal Government and the Government of Great Britain prior to the Great War for the protection of commerce in the destruction of derelicts, has reached this office by reference.

"**2.** In reply I beg to state that Article VI of the International Convention for the Safety of Life at Sea, which was signed by the delegates of the various countries on January 20, 1914, provided for an international service of derelict destruction, study and observation of ice conditions, and an ice patrol.

"**3.** Article VII of this convention invited the United States to undertake this international service, and provided that the high contracting powers which were interested in this international service contribute to the expense of maintaining this international service in certain proportions.

"**4.** While Article VI of the convention provided that the new international service should be established with the least possible delay, the convention, as a whole, could not come into force until July 1, 1915, and if the organization of the international service were deferred until after that date, the consequence would be that the two ice seasons of the years 1914 and 1915 would not be covered by the proposed international ice patrol, and, therefore, the British Government, acting on behalf of the other maritime powers, requested the United States to begin this international ice patrol and observation without delay and under the same conditions as provided in the convention. The President directed this to be done, and the Coast Guard undertook the work and performed the ice patrol during the seasons of 1914, 1915, and 1916. It was intended that the Coast Guard should also undertake the international service of derelict destruction at the conclusion of the ice patrol each year, but owing to the outbreak of the war in Europe in 1914, the international service of derelict destruction was never begun.

"**5.** As pointed out above, the international ice patrol and ice observation service was begun in 1914 and was continued during 1915 and 1916, but for obvious reasons the patrol was discontinued in 1917 and has not as yet been resumed.

"**6.** Of course, as you are aware, the various Coast Guard cutters recover or destroy such derelicts as may be found within a reasonable distance of our coast.

"**7.** I am sending you under separate cover a copy of the International Convention for the Safety of Life at Sea, also copies of Revenue-Cutter Service Bulletins Nos. 1, 3, and 5, covering reports of ice patrol for the years 1913, 1914, and 1915, respectively. The report of the ice patrol for 1916 has not yet been published.

"Respectfully,
"(Signed) E. P. Bertholf,
"Commodore Commandant."

Lost Liners

About forty years ago the fine British barque *David G. Worth*, commanded by Capt. Thomas Williams, and owned by the writer, James Sprunt, sailed from Wilmington, N. C., with a full cargo of naval stores bound for the United Kingdom. The owner had spent $10,000 for extensive repairs in London on the previous voyage, and the ship was in every respect staunch and strong and classed A1 Lloyd's and 3/3 II French Veritas. The captain's wife accompanied him, and the crew numbered sixteen.

From the day of her departure from Wilmington bound to Bristol up to the present time, not a word, not a sign of her, has ever come to light. As Mr. Joseph Horner said in *Lost Liners:*

> *"We only know she sailed away*
> *"And ne'er was seen or heard of more."*

"Lost absolutely, in the fullest and most awful sense of the term! Swallowed up wholly, mysteriously, by the devouring sea! Such has been the fate of many gallant ships; no single survivor to tell the story; no boat or piece of wreckage, no bottle, not a sign or syllable from the vasty deep to reveal the nature of the awful catastrophe by which vessel, cargo, crew, and passengers were blotted out of existence! There is a weirdness, an awful terror, in such mysterious disappearances. They fill the imagination with horror, and cause mental tension in the minds of relatives of the lost far harder to bear than when the fate of a wrecked vessel is told by survivors. The sinking of the *Royal Charter*, or of the *London*, or of the *Northfleet*, though gruesome and harrowing, does not produce in the mind that sense of pain which comes with the recollection of the fate of the *President*, or of the *Pacific*, or of the *City of Boston.*"

Continuing, Mr. Horner in *Chambers's Journal* says: "The number of vessels which have so mysteriously disappeared at sea that not a trace of them or of their crew or passengers has ever been found is larger than most people imagine. In the North Atlantic service alone, from the year 1841, when the *President* disappeared with 136 souls, to 1890, when the *Thanemore* of the Johnston Line, with 43 lives, never came to port, there have been, inclusive of these, no fewer than 24 big steamers absolutely and completely blotted out of human knowledge, together with their crews and passengers, numbering in all 1,453. At a very moderate estimate, the value of these vessels with their cargoes could not have been less than £5,000,000. The sum of human agony involved is terrible to contemplate. And every year vessels are posted up as missing.

"The *President*, one of the earliest Atlantic liners, was the first steamer to be lost and never heard of again. She sailed from New York on the 11th of March, 1841, with 136 souls on board. She was a nearly new vessel, having left the Mersey on her first voyage on the 17th of July, 1840. The commander was Lieutenant Roberts, R. N., a man of iron will and resource. He had taken the *Sirius* on her first voyage from Queenstown to New York in 1838 in eighteen and a half days. The *Sirius* was the first steamer owned by an English company which crossed the Atlantic, and but for the determination of Lieutenant Roberts the crew would not have proceeded; they became mutinous, and said it was utter madness to go on in so small a craft. He insisted and had resort to firearms, and so brought the little vessel to her destination.

"After the loss of the *President* in 1841, thirteen years elapsed in which only one life was lost by the wreck of an Atlantic steamer. It is a curious coincidence that, after the *President* was lost and never heard of, the next great loss of life, which occurred in 1854, was also that of a vessel which disappeared without leaving a trace. This was the *City of Glasgow*, which sailed with 480 souls on board. The *Pacific*, of the Collins Line, left Liverpool on the 29th of June, 1856, and with her living freight of 240 was never more heard of. In the year 1859 an Anchor liner, the *Tempest*, mysteriously disappeared with 150 souls. The *City of Boston* of the Inman Line, with 177 persons, was never heard of after leaving port on the 28th of January, 1870. A board stating that she was sinking was found in Cornwall on February 11, 1870. The Allan liner *Huronian* left Glasgow in February, 1902, for St. John's and disappeared. The British gunboat *Condor* was lost in the Pacific in 1901. Besides these, the names of many lesser-known vessels swell the long list of tragic disappearances.

"The White Star cattle steamer *Naronic*, with a crew of sixty hands and seventeen cattlemen, was lost in February or March, 1893, while on a voyage from Liverpool to New York. She was a month overdue before very much anxiety was felt, as it was known that heavy weather had been experienced in the Atlantic, and it was thought that she might have broken down and was making for the Azores. A boat with the name *Naronic* on it was subsequently found half full of water and abandoned. In this case the vessel was a new one, launched in May of the previous year. She was built with bulkheads and all modern improvements, was 460 feet long, and had engines of 3,000 horsepower. Yet she disappeared, perhaps 1,500 miles from New York, that being the location of the abandoned boat."

Probably the most mysterious disappearance of recent times is that of the United States collier transport *Cyclops*, which sailed from Barbados for Baltimore March 4, 1918, and has not been heard of since. The official information respecting this important vessel is fragmentary and disconnected. In December, 1917, she reached Bahia, Brazil, and was ordered to take on a cargo of manganese at Rio de Janeiro for the return voyage. The Navy Department exchanged several messages regarding her cargo with the commander in chief of the Pacific fleet, and, on February 7, the latter sent the following message concerning damage to one of her engines:

"Starboard high pressure engine found to be damaged on board *U.S.S. Cyclops* during passage Bahia, Brazil, to Rio de Janeiro. Board of investigation reports accident due to loosening of nuts on follower ring studs, resulting in breaking of follower ring. Cylinder is broken into two parts by plane of fracture passing from inboard upper edge down and outboard at angle of about 45 degrees. Cylinder cover and piston ring broken

U.S.S. Cyclops, *a navy collier, as she appeared in this 1911 photo.*

and piston rod bent just below piston, which is damaged. So far as now determined, responsibility seems to be upon engineer officer watch Lieut. L. J. Fingleton, who did not stop engines nor report noise. Board recommends that new cylinder, piston rod and piston, piston rings and follower be manufactured. That cylinder cover be repaired by welding upon return United States. Repair of cylinder by welding believed possible. Can not be made here. Engine compounded and vessel will proceed thus when loaded."

She reached Barbados safely and began her voyage from there to Baltimore. Being overdue, the Navy Department sent the following message to the naval stations at Key West, Charleston, Guantanamo, Navy Radio San Juan, and the *U.S.S. Albert:*

March 22, 1918.
"U.S.S. Cyclops sailed from Barbados March 4 for Baltimore. Now about ten days overdue. Endeavor communicate Cyclops by radio and ascertain location and condition."

The following day the Navy Department sent a similar message to the commander of Squadron I, Patrol Force, Atlantic fleet. On March 24 the station at Charleston, S. C., reported that at intervals for twenty-three hours messages by radio had been sent in an endeavor to locate the *Cyclops*, but without success. Commander Belknap directed that calls be continued, and on March 26 the Navy Department sent the following message to the Governor of the Virgin Islands:

"U.S.S. Cyclops sailed from Barbados March 4 for Baltimore. Has not yet arrived. Have you any information regarding this vessel passing St. Thomas?"

The reply was *"No information regarding U.S.S. Cyclops."*

Every station within radio communication of her route and every ship within call during the time of her passage, including foreign ships, was asked for any fragment of information. The search was continued as long as it seemed possible to gain news of her, but nothing definite was ever heard. The only suggestion of how she may have been lost is contained in a message to the Navy Department from the First Naval District, received June 6, 1918:

"Mr. Freeman, now in Boston, telephone address held in this office, states log of U.S.S. Amalco shows that on night of March 9 U.S.S. Cyclops was about five miles distant. March 10 heavy gale damaged the Amalco. Capt. C. E. Hilliard, of the Amalco, now at 2876 Woodbrook Avenue, Baltimore, Md."

On April 22 the commander in chief of the Pacific fleet sent to the Navy Department the following statement of her cargo:

"U.S.S. Cyclops had by tally of bucket 10,604, by draft in feet 10,835 tons manganese, distributed number one hold 1,614; number two hold 1,995; number three 2,250; number four 1,875; number five 2,870. Cargo stowed direct on wood dunnage in bottom of hold. Reports differ as to whether cargo was trimmed level or left somwhat higher in middle. Incline to latter belief. Reported also vessel had 4,000 tons of water, mostly in double bottoms. So far as ascertained, no steps taken to prevent increasing of metacentric height, and this must have been considerably increased."

What caused the catastrophe will probably never be known, but with one of her engines reported out of order she was not in the best condition to weather the storm reported by the *Amalco*, and it is not unlikely that a sudden shifting of her cargo caused her to capsize and to be instantly engulfed.

Exactly one hundred days from the date of her sailing the following order was issued:

"From: Secretary of the Navy.
"To: Bureau of Medicine and Surgery (via Bureau of Navigation).
"Subject: Re official declaration of death of men on board the Navy collier *Cyclops.*

"**I.** The following named enlisted men in the U. S. Navy and Marine Corps should be officially declared dead as of June 14, 1918, deaths having occurred in the line of duty through no misconduct of their own:"
(Here followed a list of the crew and passengers of the Navy collier Cyclops at the time of disappearance.)

"(Signed) Franklin D. Roosevelt,
"Acting Secretary of the Navy."

In his annual report for 1918 the Secretary of the Navy states "*Cyclops* was finally given up as lost and her name stricken from the registry."

Causes of the Destruction of Lost Ships

S ince the veil that conceals the catastrophes that sent the missing
vessels to their doom can never be lifted, a wide field of surmise is
open. We can only guess at the causes of these losses by considering
what has taken place in the case of vessels which have received serious
injuries the nature of which is known. I quote Mr. Horner in giving the
following as the possible causes which may account for the total
disappearance of liners: "Capsizing; damage from within, as explosion,
breakdown of machinery, or fire; damage from without, as collision with an
iceberg or with a derelict hulk; and mysterious causes.

"In reference to explosions, there are two possible causes. One is due
to the steam boilers, the other to coal gas generated in the bunkers.
Accidents from both causes have frequently occurred; and though it is not
easy to see how the force could be sufficiently great to rend a vessel asunder
without affording time for the use of boats or life-saving appliances, yet the
possibility must be admitted. Boilers are always in the bottom of the vessel,
and it is quite conceivable that one or more boiler explosions would rupture
the sides and let the water in in large volumes. In the case of a tug in the

harbor at Cardiff this actually happened. And although the loss of no big vessel has been traced to this cause, it must be admitted that the cause would be sufficient, and the end would be sudden.

"Explosions of coal gas have occurred; and in past years, when less attention was paid to ventilation than at the present time and when vessels were built of wood, it is within the bounds of possibility that an explosion might have torn a hole or started planks, or might have given rise to a fire of large extent. If to this is added the terror of rough weather at night, when most of those on board would be asleep, the chances of any vestige remaining would be slender.

"Breakdowns of machinery alone would hardly account for the loss of vessels, but they might do so indirectly—first, by leaving a vessel exposed to the mercy of rough weather; secondly, by damaging the hull and letting the water in. Fractures of propeller shafts or of propeller blades are not infrequent occurrences. Neither is damage to a rudder. It is quite conceivable that a vessel disabled thus for several days and encountering exceptionally heavy weather, might be overwhelmed by the sheer force of the waves. In rough weather the chance of a disabled vessel being seen in mid-Atlantic if she drifts out of the regular routes is very slender. Steamers for many years past have been entirely dependent on their machinery, having no sails to fall back on. Only in recent years have the most modern and best liners been fitted with twin screws and double sets of engines, one of which remains

Watertight compartments kept the **City of Paris** *afloat until help arrived.*

available if the other is damaged. A disabled vessel might, therefore, in the past have suffered badly if she drifted out of the trade routes, and might have gone down in bad weather.

"Damage to machinery may also be sufficient to explain the loss of a vessel by causing her to sink at once. The *City of Paris*, of the Inman Line, had a big smash in one of her engine rooms on the 25th of March, 1890. She was coming home in fine weather, and when she was near the Irish coast the starboard engines broke down in consequence of the fracture of the starboard propeller shaft, and the sea filled the engine room. Then the massive fragments of the wrecked engine hammering against the bulkhead smashed that and allowed the water to flow into the engine room, completely filling that also. In about ten minutes both engine rooms were filled with water, adding 3,000 tons to the vessel's weight. Yet she still floated securely, and the outer skin was not damaged in the least. The water-tight compartments kept the *City of Paris* afloat for three days until help came to tow her into Queenstown. At Queenstown the openings in the sea connections of the vessel were closed with the assistance of divers. The water was pumped out of the engine rooms, and with her port engines and one screw the vessel renewed her voyage and went on safely and quietly to Liverpool without harm to anyone. In the case of the P. and O. steamer *Delhi,* which stranded on December 12, 1911, off Cape Spartel, on the Morocco coast, all the passengers were rescued, including the Duke of Fife and the Princess Royal and her daughters.

"Capsizing is not so likely a cause as some others, but it is possible. The *Captain* capsized, with the loss of hundreds of lives. The type was, however, very different from that of the liner. But the draught of a vessel diminishes toward the close of her voyage, as coal is reduced. Some vessels are unsteady, and it is conceivable that heavy weather, shifting cargo, and insufficient ballast may cause a vessel to roll over on her beam ends and capsize. There is little doubt that the *Wartah* capsized by reason of top-heaviness. One of her life buoys was reported as being found (December, 1911) at Waiuku, New Zealand.

"But the most probable cause of unexplained losses of ships at sea is fire, or it is one, at least, which divides probabilities with explosions and icebergs. Even on the supposition of an explosion, it seems almost inexplicable that no trace of a sunken vessel should ever afterwards be seen. A missing liner or other large vessel is a source of interest to all seafaring men, and a keen outlook is kept on the track which the vessel was known to have taken. Any stray spar or belt or bit of wreckage, therefore, could scarcely escape observation. If a vessel sinks in mid-ocean some portions float. But if a vessel is burned everything would probably be consumed, as the vessel would burn to the water's edge. Boats might or might not be launched, according to the rapidity of the rush of the flames, the state of the weather, etc. If boats are launched, say, a thousand miles from land, the chances of rescue or of making land are remote. Fire, therefore, seems adequate enough to account for the loss of some of the numerous vessels which have never been heard from after leaving port.

"Considering other possible external causes of the total disappearance of liners, heavy weather must be regarded as a probable reason in some instances. Although we do not admit that the roughest weather would harm a modern liner, we must remember that the older vessels were not as large and powerful as those of the present time. The *Pacific*, for example, which disappeared in 1856, was not nearly half the length of the latest vessels. Bulkheads had not been brought to the perfect condition of security which they have now attained. Not infrequently even now steamers become water-logged and reach a sinking condition and their crews are happy if rescued. It may well have happened that vessels have foundered in mid-ocean in consequence of not being able to receive assistance, while the sailors could not take to their boats with any hope of living in the tempest.

"Uncharted rocks also cause the loss of vessels, as in the case of the *Pericles*. But her captain was a man of resource and no lives were lost.

"Icebergs are a probable cause for the loss of some vessels, especially of liners running to Canadian ports. The damage to the *Arizona* may be instanced, and many other vessels have had hair-breadth escapes. A vessel insufficiently secured by bulkheads would stand a poor chance in collision with an iceberg.

"Tidal waves are probably accountable for some unexplained losses. There are three classes of such waves—those due to submarine seismical disturbances, solitary waves occurring in an otherwise calm sea (the origin of which is obscure), and cyclonic waves. Each is very dangerous, the first and last chiefly in the vicinity of coasts, the second out at sea. It was a seismic wave which wrought such havoc at Lisbon in 1755 and in Japan in 1896, when 30,000 people were killed. But the effects of these do not usually extend far out to sea, as do those of solitary waves. Many records of the latter have been given where the decks of vessels have been swept of all hands and of all deck erections. In 1881 all hands were washed off the decks

The Cunard Line's Etruria *was hammered by a tidal wave in 1903.*

of the *Rosario.* In 1882 the master and half the crew of the *Loch Torridon* were swept off the deck by a tidal wave. In 1887 the *Umbria* was flooded by two great waves. In 1894 the *Normania* was struck by a solid wall of water reaching as high as the bridge, smashing the cabin on the promenade deck, and carrying away the music room and the officers' quarters. The height of tidal waves ranges from forty to eighty feet. The Cunarder *Etruria* was struck by a tidal wave on the 10th of October, 1903, when a Canadian gentleman was killed and several wounded. The captain's port bridge and stanchions were carried away. Though such waves would not greatly endanger the huge modern liners, they might have swamped their predecessors by breaking through the decks or rushing down hatchways and skylights. Many vessels have been lost by being pooped by vast storm waves, which are not as high as many tidal waves.

"In reference to mysterious agencies, these can be dismissed in the present state of knowledge. The secrets of the sea have been investigated so well that no destructive agent is likely to exist that is not known to science. Collision with a whale would not damage a liner, though it would be bad for the whale. The sea serpent may be dismissed without comment. The eruption of submarine volcanoes may be dangerous to small vessels, but the idea of

The **C.S.S. Chickamauga,** *which Sprunt saw at Nova Scotia in 1864.*

harm from them can not be entertained in connection with the Atlantic service. So that, after all, we are driven back for the solution of these disappearances to the same causes which are known to have wrecked so many vessels. Among these must be included collision with derelict wrecks, which have been known to drift about in the Atlantic for over a twelvemonth, and unhappily the malicious placing of explosives among the cargoes of liners, as was done at Bremerhaven in 1875."

During the War between the States, on the 24th of August, 1864, the writer was captured after bombardment for five hours while serving as purser of the Confederate steamer *Lilian*, engaged in running the Federal blockade off Wilmington, N. C., and made a prisoner of war. Subsequently he escaped to Halifax, Nova Scotia, and reported to a prominent citizen of that town who was acting as the Confederate States representative. He was one of the most popular Southern sympathizers; a man of fine presence, good business qualifications, courteous and amiable to a degree. He was trusted by all, and he acted as banker for nearly every Southerner who came his way. Halifax was then the center of large Confederate interests. Several Confederate war steamers were there, among them the *Chickamauga* and the *Tallahassee*. It was the rendezvous of blockade runners who had escaped from confinement or who had been discharged after detention by the Federals for several months. K— was attentive to all of them. When the war ended K— suddenly disappeared with the cash entrusted to him by confiding Confederates.

Several years after, there was a great explosion upon the dock where a German mail steamer was loading for sea which produced a sensation throughout the world. An infernal machine intended to wreck the liner had prematurely exploded on the quay and killed and maimed a large number of persons, among whom was the shipper, under an assumed name. This man, mortally wounded, was eagerly questioned by the police as to his diabolical plans and his accomplices; the only clue they obtained from his incoherent ravings was an intimation that he had been connected in some way with the Confederacy, and strangely enough he said something about Captain Maffitt and my ship the *Lilian*. The authorities took photographs of him, which were imperfect because of the reclining position of the dying man. Further investigation after his death revealed one of the most fiendish plots in commercial history; large shipments of bogus goods had been made by the liner, and heavily insured by this stranger, who had designed a clock machine intended, it was said, to explode three days after the sailing of the steamer, and sink her with all on board. For many months the secret service detectives were working on this case; at length one of them came to Wilmington and questioned me about the man, whose picture was exhibited. Neither I nor any of the pilots at Smithville could identify him, although his face was strangely familiar to me. The detective went away, but returned in a few weeks and asked me if I had known a man named K—. "Yes," I at once replied, "and he was the author of this awful crime." Such proved to be the case. It was the old story of depraved associates and the downward road to ruin.

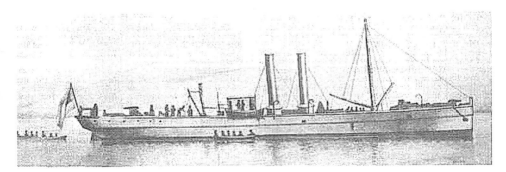

C.S.S. Tallahassee, *the other notable Confederate war steamer the author saw in* **Halifax.**

To The Rescue

I have said in *Chronicles of the Cape Fear River*, pages 525-527, that a public service which measures its efficiency by the number of human lives saved from the perils of the sea is to be classed among the highest humanities of a great government, and that an important arm of great reach and efficiency is the admirable service of the *U.S.S. Seminole* on this station.

The activities of this ship in assisting vessels in distress are so continuous as to be classed by her efficient commander as all in the day's work. In the four months from December 1, 1912, this ship assisted nine vessels in distress at sea and destroyed a tenth, the *Savannah*, a dangerous derelict.

A typical case is described in the recent rescue in a gale of wind three hundred miles off Cape Fear, of the British mail and passenger steamer *Korona*, bound from St. Thomas, West Indies, for New York, whose boilers broke down, rendering the ship helpless without motive power, wallowing in a heavy sea which threatened to engulf her.

The story of this splendid rescue of a hundred human lives is told in the matter-of-fact official report of Capt. Eugene Blake, Jr., of the *Seminole*, and in the letter of thanks to the Secretary of the Navy, which follows, with the Acting Secretary's reply:

"Wilmington, N. C.,
"*April 2, 1919.*
"*Seminole.*

"**From:** Commanding Officer.
"**To:** Commandant, Fifth Naval District.
"**Subject:** Report of search and tow of Canadian S. S. *Korona.*

"**1.** At 1 a.m. on the morning of March 25, the following message was transmitted to the *Seminole* from the communication officer at district headquarters:
" 'March 24, 1919: *Korona* boilers out of commission. Needs assistance. Position, latitude 31-48 N., longitude 72-12 W., noon, today. Signed, Doyle, Master.'
"**2.** The *Seminole* left the Berkley oil docks at 7 a. m. the same morning and proceeded at top speed for the reported position of the *Korona*,

The U.S. Revenue Cutter Seminole *took the* Korona *in tow.*

passing through the Gulf Stream from 2 a. m. to 8 a.m. of the morning of March 26.

"**3.** At 8 a.m. in the forenoon of March 26, intercepted a radiogram from the Porto Rican S. S. Co.'s steamer *Coamo* that she had the *Korona* in tow, and was proceeding with her to the westward. Communication by radio was immediately established with the *Coamo*, and the position, course, and speed ascertained. It was also learned that as the *Coamo* was bound to the southward for Porto Rico, she was anxious to be relieved of the tow. Arrangements were therefore made to meet the *Coamo* at the nearest possible meeting point and at 10 that morning the course of both vessels was changed to effect this meeting at about 7 that evening. The *Seminole* was run under forced draft in order to take advantage of the weather, which was then favorable to picking up the disabled vessel.

"**4.** At 6.45 p.m. March 26, the *Coamo* with *Korona* in tow was sighted bearing almost dead ahead, and at 8.15 p.m. the *Coamo* had been relieved of the tow and the *Seminole's* hawser shackled into the starboard chain of the *Korona*. The *Korona's* master stated that his port of destination was New York and requested to be towed to the northward. Hampton Roads was accordingly selected as the port of destination and the course shaped for Diamond Shoals buoy.

"**5.** The weather, which up to this time had been fine, commenced to show signs of a decided change, and the storm warning received the following morning, March 27, confirmed the prediction of an approaching gale. The wind, however, was from southwest to south, and, being favorable, good progress was made, at an estimated speed of five or six knots from the time the *Korona* was picked up until midnight of March 27.

"**6.** By this time the wind had shifted to west and was blowing a strong gale, and the *Seminole* was unable to hold up to her course with the tow. We were shipping heavy seas at frequent intervals and were practically hove to and drifting to leeward. About 2 a m. March 28, the wind shifted to northwest with slightly increased force, and the *Seminole* was put before the gale with engines turning over at dead slow speed, sufficient to keep the *Korona* astern, to act as a drag. This is an unfavorable position for the *Seminole* because she rolls to a dangerous angle in a following sea and takes much water in the waist, but it was the best that could be accomplished under the circumstances. The tow semed to be fairly comfortable.

"**7.** During the night of March 27 and daylight of March 28, the *Seminole* with tow lost about 60 miles in a general southeasterly direction.

"**8.** On March 28, picked up an S.O.S. call from the steamer *Alapaha* in our immediate vicinity; in fact this steamer reported herself in sight at one time during the day, but as she was going to leeward faster than the *Seminole* and reported no immediate danger to her crew, there seemed no reason for abandoning one vessel for a doubtful chance of picking up the other. It was also learned that the Coast Guard cutter *Yamacraw* was proceeding to her assistance.

"**9.** The weather moderated slightly during the afternoon of March 28, and at 5.40 p.m. the *Seminole* with tow was brought up head to wind and sea on course northwest, making little if any progress. The gale increased again in force from 8 p.m. to midnight, and at 3 a.m. March 29 west was the best heading that could be held.

"**10.** During the worst of the gale this night the *Seminole's* air pump stopped, and the two vessels fell off into the trough of the sea and at one time were in imminent danger of collision. The *Seminole* being the lighter and naturally in the weather position, drifted faster than the *Korona*, but was worked clear by setting the staysails and getting a few turns out of the engine at the critical moment. As soon as the *Seminole* was to leeward of the *Korona*, the engine was stopped and in the course of an hour the air pump was repaired.

"**11.** The northwest weather continuing throughout March 29 with gale force, it was decided to make Wilmington, N.C., and a westerly course was maintained throughout the day.

"**12.** About 2 p.m. on March 30 the *Korona* managed to get a small head of steam on one boiler, and, after coupling up propeller, which had been disconnected on taking up the tow, was able to turn her engine over at slow speed. This materially lightened the weight of the tow and we were able to make way at a speed between four and five knots.

"**13.** Continued at this rate of speed through March 30 and 31 with very slowly moderating weather, and at 1.40 p.m. on the 31st got on sounding, sighting Frying Pan Shoal buoy at 5.30 p.m. that date.

"**14.** During the night of March 31 a moderate northerly gale developed, but the tow, being under the lee of Frying Pan Shoal, was easily manageable. Speed was regulated to arrive off Cape Fear River entrance at daylight, and upon reaching that point the heavy hawser was unshackled and the *Korona* towed up the river to Wilmington with a lighter line and short scope.

"**15.** Arrived off Wilmington at 2.30 p.m., where *Korona* was turned over to her agents, Alexander Sprunt & Sons Co., the *Seminole* proceeding to her wharf at the custom-house.

"**16.** A Coast Guard statistical report of this assistance is attached.

"Eugene Blake, Jr."

"April 2, 1919.

"Sir: As agents in Wilmington, N. C., of the Quebec Steamship Co., owners of the British steamer *Korona*, as agents of Lloyds, as agents of the London Salvage Association, and as official agents of the British Ministry of Shipping, and in behalf of Capt. Austin Doyle, his officers and crew and passengers of the British steamer *Korona*, numbering in all a hundred persons, we desire to express to you and to Captain Blake, his officers and crew of the *U.S.S. Seminole*, through you, our deep sense of gratefulness for the rescue from imminent peril in a heavy sea of the disabled steamer *Korona* while on her voyage from St. Thomas to New York; and for their splendid seamanship in averting collision and in towing her under great difficulties to this port of refuge.

"Tossed upon a raging sea without motive power, the *Korona* was in great danger, and her rescue after four days' continuous assistance adds another high record of splendid achievement by the *U.S.S. Seminole* and her devoted men.

"Permit us, Sir, to thank you cordially in the names of all concerned for this added admirable and effective example of the highest degree of humanity and efficiency in an important arm of the U.S. Navy.

"Yours very respectfully,
"(Signed) Alexander Sprunt & Son.
"To the Honorable Josephus Daniels,
"The Secretary of the Navy,
"Washington, D. C."

"Navy Department,
"Washington, April 7, 1919.

"Dear Sirs:

Receipt is acknowledged of your letter of April 2, expressing gratitude for the rescue of the disabled steamer *Korona* by the *U.S.S. Seminole*.

"Your letter of appreciation has been forwarded to the commanding officer of the *U.S.S. Seminole* via the Commodore Commandant of the Coast Guard Service and the Commandant of the Fifth Naval District, under whose orders the *U.S.S. Seminole* is operating.

"It is a great pleasure to know that the work of our salvage and rescue ships is appreciated, and I thank you very sincerely for your expression of thanks and recognition of the excellent seamanship and devotion to duty shown by the captain, officers, and crew of the *U.S.S. Seminole*.

"Very truly yours,
"(Signed) Franklin D. Roosevelt,
"*Acting Secretary of the Navy.*

"Messrs. Alexander Sprunt & Son,
"*Wilmington, North Carolina.*"

Derelict Blockade Runners

For many years the summer visitors on Wrightsville Beach have looked out upon the hurrying swell of the broad Atlantic and have felt the fascination of the long lines of crested breakers like Neptune's racers charging and reforming for the never-ending fray; and, when the unresting tide receded, they have seen the battered hulks of some of the most beautiful ships that ever shaped a course for Wilmington in the days of the Southern Confederacy. They represented an epoch that is unique in our country's history, for, in the modern art of war the conditions which then prevailed can never occur again.

Some of these wrecks may be visible for a hundred years to come, and, as nearly every one who knew these vessels and of their last voyage has passed away, I have thought it might interest some of our people, and perhaps future generations, to know something of these ships, which I still remember distinctly and with whose officers I was more or less familiar. So that I have noted from memory and from official records of the Four Years' War, the tragedies which involved the destruction of these fine vessels between Topsail Inlet and Lockwood's Folly. These will comprise about thirty ships, nearly all of the steamers that were stranded on our coast during the war while running for the Cape Fear Bar under a heavy bombardment by the Federal cruisers.

Many millions were lost with the destruction of these blockade runners, and possibly valuable metal might be recovered now, in the present high prices for all war supplies. The average cost of one of the blockade runners was $150,000 in gold. They were mostly built of thick iron, which does not corrode like steel in salt water.

The cargoes comprised perishable and imperishable goods, and they were often as valuable as the vessels which carried them. When these ships

George Davis

were stranded so high upon the beach that neither Federals nor Confederates could salve them, the guns from both sides were used to destroy them, so that neither could profit by a rescue. The bombshells set some of the ships on fire, but none were totally destroyed, because the breakers extinguished the fires when the superstructure was burned away, so it is very probable that some of them still contain cargoes of value.

For more than fifty years these melancholy tokens of distress have settled in the shifting sands.

"Together," said Mr. George Davis, Attorney-General of the Confederacy, "they stand for warning and for woe; and together they catch the long majestic roll of the Atlantic as it sweeps through a thousand miles of grandeur and power from the Arctic toward the Gulf. It is the playground of billows and tempests, the kingdom of silence and awe, disturbed by no sound save the seagull's shriek and the breakers' roar."

It might be interesting to add later an account of the ships that were captured at sea, numbering over a hundred during the four years of the Cape Fear blockade, and to attempt, at the request of my friend, Professor deRoulhac Hamilton, of the University of North Carolina, a short history of this remarkable traffic (through the beleaguered city of Wilmington) which almost wholly sustained the Confederate States commissariat during the last two years of the war.

The *Fannie and Jennie*

The *Fannie and Jennie* was a side-wheel Confederate steamer of note, engaged in running the blockade for about a year during the Four Years' War. She was of good speed, fourteen knots, and was commanded, it is said, by Captain Coxetter, of Charleston. During the night of February 9, 1864, she made the land to the northward of Wrightsville Beach, but her pilot, Burriss, was not sure of his position, so he anchored the ship and made a landing in the surf to ascertain his bearings. It having been the intention of the captain to make the land about two miles north of Fort Fisher, he then proceeded down the beach in the darkness. Unhappily, however, she stood too close in shore, and grounded repeatedly, and at about midnight stranded on a shoal a mile or two to the southward of where Lumina now stands. At daylight she was discovered by the Federal cruiser *Florida*, commanded by Capt. Pierce Crosby, who made me a prisoner of war a few months later. Captain Crosby, desiring to save the *Fannie and Jennie* and realize big prize money, ran a hawser from his ship to the stranded vessel, intending to pull her off into deep water, when a Confederate flying battery of Whitworth guns of long range, from Fort Fisher, opened fire from Masonboro Beach, and with great precision cut off one of the *Florida's* paddle-wheel arms, broke a second one, and cut a rim of the wheel in two; also, one of the Confederate shells exploded on board the *Florida* and came near destroying her. The *Florida* returned the fire, which so alarmed the captain and crew of the *Fannie and Jennie* that some of them attempted to reach the beach in

*The **U.S.S. Florida**, as she looked during the Civil War.*

boats. In this attempt Captain Coxetter and his purser were drowned in the breakers, the others gaining the shore; the rest of the crew, twenty-five in number, who remained on board were made prisoners by the Federals. Captain Coxetter had in his keeping a very valuable gold jewelled sword, which was to be delivered to Gen. R. E. Lee as an expression of the admiration of many prominent English sympathizers. It is still on board this wreck, which lies near a line of breakers to the south of Lumina. The *Fannie and Jennie* was loaded with a valuable cargo, five days out from Nassau bound to Wilmington, when she was stranded.

The *Emily of London*

During the month of January, 1864, while my ship was in St. George, Bermuda, loading for Wilmington, I met frequently an attractive young Virginian named Selden, of the Confederate Signal Service, who had been detailed as signal officer on the fine new steamer *Emily of London*; and I became most favorably impressed with this courteous Christian gentleman and with the superior qualities of his beautiful vessel. All of her appointments were first-class, and her equipment was superior to that of any other blockade runner of the fleet. As she lies now in sight of my cottage on Wrightsville Beach, visible at every turn of the tide, I often wonder what became of Selden, for I never learned his fate after the stranding and loss of his fine ship a mile or so above the wreck of the *Fannie and Jennie*, on the same night, February 9, 1864.

The only particulars of the stranding of the *Emily* are embodied in the official report of her discovery on the beach by Captain Crosby, of the Federal cruiser *Florida*, who found her ashore between Masonboro Inlet and Wrightsville Beach after her captain and crew had abandoned her. She was then set on fire by bombshells from the cruiser *Florida*, a loud explosion on board of the wrecked vessel indicating that her cargo was probably partly composed of explosives for the Confederacy.

Captain Crosby adds that she was a new and very handsome steamer, expensively fitted out. It is presumed that the *Emily's* captain and crew, numbering about fifty men, succeeded in reaching the protection of the Confederates.

The *Ella*

An ex-Confederate officer describing Wilmington during the blockade, among many interesting things, said the following:

"Owing to the configuration of the coast it was almost impossible to effect a close blockade. The Cape Fear had two mouths, Old Inlet, at the entrance of which Fort Caswell stands, and New Inlet, nine miles up the river, where Fort Fisher guarded the entrance. From the station off Old Inlet, where there were usually from five to six blockaders, around to the station off New Inlet, a vessel would have to make an arc of some fifty miles, owing to the Frying Pan Shoals intervening, while from Caswell across to Fisher was only nine miles. The plan of the blockade runners coming in was to strike the coast thirty or forty miles above or below the inlets, and then run along (of course at night) until they got under the protection of the forts. Sometimes they got in or out by boldly running through the blockading fleet, but that was hazardous; for, if discovered, the ocean was alive with rockets and lights, and it was no pleasant thing to have shells and balls whistling over you and around you. The chances were then that if you were not caught you had, in spite of your speed, to throw a good many bales of cotton overboard.

"The wreck of these blockade runners not infrequently occurred by being stranded or beached, and highly diverting skirmishes would occur between the blockaders and the garrisons of the forts for the possession. The fleet, however, never liked the Whitworth guns we had, which shot almost with the accuracy of a rifle and with a tremendous range. The soldiers generally managed to wreck the stranded vessel successfully, though often-times with great peril and hardship. It mattered very little to the owners then who got her, as they did not see much of what was recovered—the soldiers thinking they were entitled to what they got at the risk of their lives. But a wreck was a most demoralizing affair. The whole garrison generally got drunk and stayed drunk for a week or so afterwards. Brandy and fine wines flowed like water; and it was a month perhaps before matters could be got straight. Many accumulated snug little sums from the misfortunes of the blockade runners, who generally denounced such pillage as piracy; but it could not be helped.

"We recollect the wrecking of the *Ella*, off Bald Head, in December, 1864. She belonged to the Bee Company, of Charleston, and was a splendid new steamer, on her second trip in, with a large and valuable cargo almost entirely owned by private parties and speculators. She was chased ashore by the blockading fleet, and immediately abandoned by her officers and crew, whom nothing would induce to go back in order to save her cargo. Yankee shells flying over, and through, and around her, had no charms for these sons of Neptune. Captain Badham, however, and his company, the Edenton (N. C.) Battery, with Captain Bahnson, a fighting Quaker from Salem, N. C., boarded and wrecked her under the fire of the Federals, six shells passing through the *Ella* while they were removing her cargo. The consequence was that for a month afterwards nearly the whole garrison was on 'a tight,' and groceries and dry goods were plentiful in that vicinity. The general demoralization produced by 'London Dock' and 'Hollands' seemed even to have affected that holy man, the chaplain, who said some very queer graces at the headquarters mess table."

The *Modern Greece*

One of the earliest strandings of friendly steamers near New Inlet, or Cape Fear main bar, was that of the *Modern Greece*, which was also the most important and interesting. On the morning of the 27th of June, 1862, at 4.15 o'clock the *Modern Greece* had safely evaded many Federal cruisers and was within three miles of Fort Fisher, headed for New Inlet, when she was seen by one of the Federal blockaders, the *Cambridge*, which immediately gave chase and pelted the *Modern Greece* with bombshells. The *Cambridge* was joined by the Federal cruiser *Stars and Stripes*, which also opened fire on the *Modern Greece*, the latter being then run ashore to avoid capture, her crew escaping in their boats to the shore. In the meantime Fort Fisher was firing at the enemy and also at the *Modern Greece* where she was stranded, in order to prevent the Federals from hauling her off. The crew of the *Modern Greece* was in great peril during this bombardment, as part of her valuable cargo consisted of a thousand tons of powder for the Confederacy and many guns. The garrison at Fort Fisher subsequently landed a large

*The **Modern Greece** hard aground and being salvaged by Confederate troops.*

The **U.S.S. Cambridge,** *the ship that chased down the* **Modern Greece.**

amount of clothing and barrels of spirits, and the spirits flowed like water for several weeks to the scandal of the fort and its defenders. Its potent influence was also felt in Wilmington. The *Modern Greece* was a large British propeller of about 1,000 tons net register, one of the largest blockade runners of the war. She now lies deep in the sand near Fort Fisher.

The *Elizabeth*

One of the regular passenger and freight boats which ran between New Orleans and Galveston before the war was named *Atlantic*. She became a famous blockade runner under her original name, which was changed later to *Elizabeth*.

I think she was commanded for several voyages by the celebrated Capt. Thomas J. Lockwood of Southport and Charleston, whose capable brother-in-law, George C. McDougal, was her chief engineer. Mr. McDougal was a man of fine qualities, quiet and retiring in his demeanor. He made in various steamers sixty successful runs through the blockade. For more than twenty-five years after the war I enjoyed the privilege of his intimate confidences, and I have no hesitation in saying that he was to my mind the most remarkable man who had been engaged in blockade running.

On the 19th of September, 1863, the *Elizabeth* sailed from Nassau with a general cargo, mostly steel and saltpeter, bound for Wilmington, but through some unknown cause ran ashore at Lockwood's Folly, twelve miles from Fort Caswell. The captain set her on fire and burned her on the 24th, the crew escaping to the shore. A man who gave his name as Norris or Morris was captured, second officer on the *Douro*, stranded October 12, 1863, and he told the commander of the cruiser *Nansemond* that he was a Federal spy and that he was on the *Elizabeth* when she was stranded, and he exhibited eight ounces of laudanum and two ounces of chloroform which he said he bought in Nassau to put in the whisky and water of the firemen of the *Elizabeth* and of the *Douro* so as to cause the capture of these vessels, but he did not explain why the *Elizabeth* went ashore while he was in her.

The *Georgiana McCaw*

About the year 1878 there flourished in Wilmington the Historical and Literary Society, composed of about fifty eminent citizens of education and refinement. In those days our representative men found pleasure and relaxation from the drudgery of business or the strain of professional life in

Rev. Joseph Wilson

the congenial company which assembled for mutual benefit once a month in the lecture room of the Presbyterian Church on Orange Street. Such men as Doctor Wilson, father of the President, Doctor deRossett, Alfred Martin and his son E. S. Martin, who sometimes represented opposing views, Doctor Wood, Edward Cantwell, Doctor Morrelle, Alexander Sprunt, Henry Nutt, and many others, engaged in learned discussions of subjects suggested by the title of this organization.

On a certain occasion one of the gentlemen named, to whose patriotic ardor we were almost wholly indebted for the closure of New Inlet and the consequent benefit to Cape Fear commerce, rose in his usual dignified and impressive manner with an air of extraordinary importance and mystery. Said he, "Mr. Chairman, I hold in my hands a relic of prehistoric times, cast up by the heaving billows off Federal Point, formerly known as Confederate Point. It is a piece of corroded brass upon which is inscribed a legend as yet indecipherable; in all probability it long antedates the coming of Columbus."

A curious group immediately surrounded the learned member with expressions of awe and admiration, and after several speeches had been made, by resolution unanimously adopted, Mr. E. S. Martin and two other members were entrusted with the precious relic for its elucidation by conferring with the antedeluvian societies of the North.

At the following monthly meeting Mr. Martin reported for his committee that their efforts to identify the relic through reference to archeological societies in the North had been futile, but that a profane Scotchman had informed them that the piece of metal was no more than a part of the bow or stern escutcheon of the stranded blockade runner *Georgiana McCaw*, the palm tree in the center surrounded by the motto *Let Glasgow Flourish*, being the coat of arms of Glasgow,* Scotland, the home port of the said blockade runner. Alas! it was only another case of Bill Stubbs, his mark, but we never took the antedeluvians of the North into our confidence about it.

The official report of Acting Master Everson, U. S. Navy, commanding the Federal cruiser *Victoria*, dated off Western Bar, Wilmington, N. C., June 2, 1864, addressed to the senior officer of the blockading squadron, is as follows, with reference to the stranding of the *Georgiana McCaw:*

"Sir:

I have the honor to report that at 3 a.m., of this date, and while drifting in three and a half fathoms water, Bald Head Light bearing east, saw white water near the beach to the south and westward, which I supposed to be a steamer. I immediately steamed ahead at full speed toward the beach in order to cut her off.

"On near approach I discovered her to be a sidewheel steamer, steering for the bar.

"As he crossed my bow I rounded to in his wake and discharged at him my starboard 8-inch gun, loaded with one 5-second shell and stand of grape, and kept firing my 30-pound rifle as I continued the chase, until 3.30 a.m. she struck on the bar. I immediately ordered the first and second cutters to board and fire her, the former under command of Acting Master's Mate William Moody, the latter under charge of Acting Third Assistant Engineer Thomas W. Hineline.

"On arrival on board they found that two boats, with their crews, had escaped to the shore.

"They, however, succeeded in capturing twenty-nine of the crew, including the captain and most of the officers, together with three passengers.

"They fired her in several places, and she continued to burn until 10 a.m., when she was boarded from the shore. At daylight Fort Caswell and

---

* "Let Glasgow flourish by the preaching of the Word."

the adjacent batteries opened fire on our boats with shot and shell, which compelled them to return without accomplishing her destruction.

"She proved to be the *Georgiana McCaw* of Liverpool, 700 tons burden, from Nassau, bound to Wilmington, N. C.

"Her cargo consists of about 60 tons provisions, etc.

"I would add, sir, that too much credit can not be awarded to Acting Master's Mate William Moody and Acting Third Assistant Engineer Thomas W. Hineline for their perseverance and energy displayed, and their cool and gallant conduct while under fire of the enemy."

The *Wild Dayrell*

One of the most prominent personalities of the blockade era was Thomas E. Taylor, a young Englishman, aged twenty-one, who was sent by a wealthy Liverpool firm to direct in person the movements of steamers which

Col. William Lamb, C.S.A.

they had bought or builded for this dangerous traffic. He began with the old steamer *Dispatch*, which was found to be too slow and after one or more voyages was sent back to England. His employers then began building lighter, faster boats specially adapted to the purpose, until they owned and operated a fleet of fifteen steamers. One of them, the *Banshee*, was the first steel vessel that crossed the Atlantic, and Mr. Taylor came in her to Wilmington. His agreeable manners and courteous deportment attracted the favorable recognition of General Whiting and of Colonel Lamb, whose personal and official regard was of great value to Mr. Taylor. He wrote an interesting book after the war from which I take the following incidents in his eventful career.

"As soon as the nights were sufficiently dark we made a start for Wilmington, unfortunately meeting very bad weather and strong head winds, which delayed us; the result was that instead of making out the blockading fleet about midnight, as we had intended, when dawn was breaking there were still no signs of it. Captain Capper, the chief engineer, and I then held a hurried consultation as to what we had better do. Capper was for going to

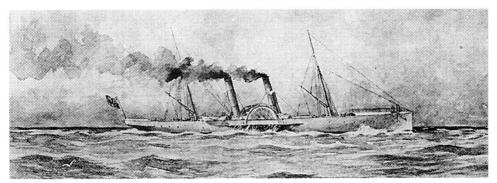

The blockade runner **Banshee,** *aboard which Tom Taylor ran for Fort Fisher.*

sea again, and if necessary returning to Nassau; the weather was still threatening, our coal supply running short, and, with a leaky ship beneath us, the engineer and I decided that the lesser risk would be to make a dash for it. 'All right,' said Capper, 'we'll go on, but you'll get d—d well peppered!'

"We steamed cautiously on, making as little smoke as possible, whilst I went to the masthead to take a look around; no land was in sight, but I could make out in the dull morning light the heavy spars of the blockading flagship right ahead of us, and soon after several other masts became visible on each side of her. Picking out what appeared to me to be the widest space between these, I signaled to the deck how to steer, and we went steadily on, determined when we found we were perceived to make a rush for it. No doubt our very audacity helped us through, as for some time they took no notice, evidently thinking we were one of their own chasers returning from sea to take up her station for the day.

"At last, to my great relief, I saw Fort Fisher just appearing above the horizon, although we knew that the perilous passage between these blockaders must be made before we could come under the friendly protection of its guns. Suddenly, we became aware that our enemy had found us out; we saw two cruisers steaming toward one another from either side of us, so as to intercept us at a given point before we could get on the land side of them. It now became simply a question of speed and immunity from being sunk by shot. Our little vessel quivered under the tremendous pressure with which she was being driven through the water.

"An exciting time followed, as we and our two enemies rapidly converged upon one point, others in the distance also hurrying up to assist them. We were now near enough to be within range, and the cruiser on our port side opened fire; his first shot carried away our flagstaff aft on which our ensign had just been hoisted; his second tore through our forehold, bulging out a plate on the opposite side. Bedding and blankets to stop the leak were at once requisitioned, and we steamed on full speed under a heavy fire from both quarters. Suddenly, puffs of smoke from the fort showed us that Colonel Lamb, the commandant, was aware of what was going on and was firing to protect us; a welcome proof that we were drawing within range of his guns and on the landward side of our pursuers, who, after giving us a few more parting shots, hauled off and steamed away from within reach of the shells which we were rejoiced to see falling thickly around them.

"We had passed through a most thrilling experience; at one time the cruiser on our port side was only a hundred yards away from us with her consort a hundred and fifty on the starboard, and it seemed a miracle that their double fire had not completely sunk us. It certainly required all one's nerve to stand upon the paddle box, looking without flinching almost into the muzzles of the guns which were firing at us; and proud we were of our crew, not a man of whom showed the white feather. Our pilot, who showed no lack of courage at the time, became, however, terribly excited as we neared the bar, and whether it was that the ship steered badly, owing to being submerged forward, or from some mistake, he ran her ashore whilst going at full speed."

On the following voyage Mr. Taylor says: "It was a critical time when daylight broke, dull and threatening. The captain was at the wheel and I at the mast-head (all other hands being employed at the pumps, and even baling), when, not four miles off, I sighted a cruiser broadside on. She turned round as if preparing to give chase, and I thought we were done for, as we could not have got more than three or four knots an hour out of our crippled boat. To my great joy, however, I found our alarm was needless, for she evidently had not seen us, and instead of heading turned her stern toward us and disappeared into a thick bank of clouds.

"Still we were far from being out of danger, as the weather became worse and worse and the wind increased in force until it was blowing almost a gale. Things began to look as ugly as they could, and even Captain Capper lost hope; I shall never forget the expression on his face as he came up to me and said, in his gruff voice, 'I say, Mr. Taylor, the beggar's going, the beggar's going,' pointing vehemently downwards. 'What the devil do you mean?' I asked. 'Why, we are going to lose the ship and our lives, too,' was the answer. It is not possible for any one unacquainted with Capper to appreciate this scene. Sturdy, thickset, nearly as broad as he was long, and with the gruffest manner but kindest heart—a rough diamond and absolutely without fear. With the exception of Steele he was the best blockade-running captain we had.

"In order to save the steamer and our lives we decided that desperate remedies must be resorted to, so again the unlucky deck cargo had to be sacrificed. The good effect of this was soon visible; we began to gain on the water, and were able, by degrees, to relight our extinguished fires. But the struggle continued to be a most severe one, for just when we began to obtain a mastery over the water the donkey engine broke down, and before we could repair it the water increased sensibly, nearly putting out our fires again. So the struggle went on for sixty hours, when we were truly thankful to steam into Nassau Harbor and beach the ship. It was a very narrow escape, for within twenty minutes after stopping her engines the vessel had sunk to the level of the water.

"After this I made a trip in a new boat that had just been sent out to me, the *Wild Dayrell*. And a beauty she was, very strong, a perfect sea boat, and remarkably well engined.

"Our voyage in was somewhat exciting, as about three o'clock in the afternoon, while making for Fort Caswell entrance (not Fort Fisher), we were sighted by a Federal cruiser that immediately gave chase. We soon found, however, that we had the heels of our friend, but it left us the alternative of going out to sea or being chased straight into the jaws of the blockaders off the bar before darkness came on. Under these circumstances what course to take was a delicate point to decide, but we solved the problem by slowing down just sufficiently to keep a few miles ahead of our chaser, hoping that darkness would come on before we made the fleet or they discovered us. Just as twilight was drawing in we made them out; cautiously we crept on, feeling certain that our enemy astern was rapidly closing up on us. Every moment we expected to hear shot whistling around us. So plainly could we see the sleepy blockaders that it seemed almost impossible we should escape their notice. Whether they did not expect a

The Federal blockade off Old Inlet in 1864, showing Fort Caswell on the left.

runner to make an attempt so early in the evening, or whether it was sheer good luck on our part, I know not, but we ran through the lot without being seen or without having a shot fired at us.

"Our anxieties, however, were not yet over, as our pilot (a new hand) lost his reckoning and put us ashore on the bar. Fortunately, the flood tide was rising fast, and we refloated, bumping over stern first in a most inglorious fashion, and anchored off Fort Caswell before 7 p.m.—a record performance. Soon after anchoring we saw a great commotion among the blockaders, who were throwing up rockets and flashing lights, evidently in answer to signals from the cruiser which had so nearly chased us into their midst.

"When we came out we met with equally good luck, as the night was pitch dark and the weather very squally. No sooner did we clear the bar than we put our helm aport, ran down the coast, and then stood boldly straight out to sea without interference; and it was perhaps as well we had such good fortune, as before this I had discovered that our pilot was of very indifferent caliber, and that courage was not our captain's most prominent characteristic. The poor *Wild Dayrell* deserved a better commander, and consequently a better fate than befell her. She was lost on her second trip, entirely through the want of pluck on the part of her captain, who ran her ashore some miles to the north of Fort Fisher; as he said, in order to avoid capture—to my mind a fatal excuse for any blockade-running captain to make. 'Twere far better to be sunk by shot and escape in the boats if possible. I am quite certain that if Steele or Capper had commanded her on that trip she would never have been put ashore, and the chances are that she would have come through all right.

"I never forgave myself for not unshipping the captain on my return to Nassau; my only excuse was that there was no good man available to replace him, and he was a particular protege of my chief. But such considerations should not have weighed, and if I had had the courage of my convictions it is probable the *Wild Dayrell* would have proved as successful as any of our steamers."

The rest of the story of the loss of the fine steamer *Wild Dayrell*, which was accidentally run ashore at Stump Inlet February 1, 1864, is told in the official report of Lieut. Commander F. A. Roe of the U.S. cruiser *Sassacus* to Admiral S. P. Lee, as follows:

The **U.S.S. Sassacus** *ramming the* **C.S.S. Albemarle** *in an earlier naval action.*

U.S.S. Sassacus
Off Stump Inlet, N. C.,
February 3, 1864.

"Sir: I have to report that about 11 o'clock a.m., on the morning of the 1st instant, in about the parallel of Topsail Inlet, N.C., I discovered a steamer close inshore, showing heavy columns of smoke. I headed for her at once, and, upon approaching, found her ashore at the mouth of Stump Inlet. Her crew were busy throwing overboard her cargo, a portion of which was scattered along the beach. When within reach of my guns, her crew and people fled in their boats, when I fired a few guns to disperse any enemies that might be hovering near. I boarded and took possession of the steamer, which proved to be the blockade runner *Wild Dayrell*. All the papers which I could find I herewith transmit. She was inward bound, two days from Nassau. I found her furnaces filled with fuel and burning, with the intention of destroying her boilers. I hauled her fires and found her machinery and the vessel in perfect order, with a portion of her cargo, consisting of assorted merchandise, still on board. I immediately got our hawsers and attempted to pull her off, but failed, owing to the falling of the tide. I made another attempt at 1 o'clock a.m. on the morning of the 2d, but parted the hawser. The weather looking bad, I put to sea until daylight, when I returned and assumed a new position to endeavor to get her off.

"In the meantime, I commenced to lighten the vessel by throwing overboard about 20 tons of coal. At high water, about 2 p.m. of the 2d, I commenced tugging at her again, when, after some time, the current sweeping me close to the shoal to leeward, the *Sassacus* struck twice lightly. I cut the hawser and steamed up to a new position and anchored. During this trial, the *U.S.S. Florida*, Commander Crosby, came in and anchored, with offers of assistance to us. During this trial the wind blew fresh from the southward and westward in heavy flaws, which was the principal cause of my failure to get her off. I then steamed up to a new position to try her again. On the 3d, while getting on board our hawsers to the prize, with the assistance of the boats of the *Florida*, my cable suddenly parted and I was forced to steam out to keep from fouling the *Florida*, which was anchored near, and in so doing parted the hauling lines of the hawsers, which were being hauled in by the *Florida's* men on board the prize.

"During this last operation the enemy appeared and opened fire with musketry upon the *Sassacus* and the boats coming from the prize. Both vessels promptly opened fire and the enemy were driven off.

"I would here observe that the cable of this vessel parted unduly, without having been strained by any swell or heavy wind, thus losing the anchor and about five fathoms of cable. We were anchored in two and three-quarter fathoms water; the cable was undoubtedly bad.

"Upon consultation with Commander Crosby we decided that it was impossible to get the steamer off, and that we must destroy her. Accordingly, I gave the signal to the men on board of her to set fire to her thoroughly and return aboard, which was done. Both vessels then opened fire upon the steamer, and she was riddled at about the water line with raking shots from the *Sassacus*. No attempt was made to save her cargo, as I deemed it impracticable to do so. Not one-half of her cargo had been thrown overboard and the rest, which I deemed very valuable merchandise, was consumed with the vessel. Valuable time would have been lost in the effort, and to pillage her would have demoralized my men for healthy action in some future similar service. Having effected this duty, I put to sea at about eight o'clock of the evening of the 3d.

"I transmit herewith an appraisement of value of the steamer and cargo, made by a board ordered upon that service.

"I have the honor to be, Sir,

"Very respectfully,
"Your obedient servant,

"F. A. Roe,
"*Lieutenant Commander.*

"Acting Rear Admiral S. P. Lee,
"*Comdg. North Atlantic Blockading Squadron, Hampton Roads.*"

The *General Beauregard*

Of the steamer *General Beauregard* I have but little information, although I remember her as a valuable ship. The *Richmond Whig* of December 16, 1863, states that according to the *Wilmington Journal* this steamer was chased ashore by the Federal blockaders on the night of the 11th instant some distance above Fort Fisher, near Battery Gatlin, and that she had been set on fire.

Captain Ridgely of the Federal cruiser *Shenandoah* (which chased my ship the *Lilian* for five hours later) reported to Admiral S. P. Lee, December 16, 1863, that on the evening of the 11th of December, 1863, between seven and eight o'clock, the cruiser *Howquah* saw the *General Beauregard* coming down the beach heading for Cape Fear or New Inlet.

Rear Admiral S.P. Lee, U.S. Navy

He gave chase and opened fire on him. The *Beauregard* being impeded by a heavy sea and finding escape impossible, ran ashore at the point already described.

The next morning the cruiser, accompanied by the *Tuscarora*, tried to board the *Beauregard*, but they were attacked by two Confederate batteries, one to the north and another to the south of the stranded vessel, and driven off, the *Tuscarora* being struck by a Confederate shell in her quarter. The *Beauregard* is still conspicuous on Carolina Beach at all stages of the tide, showing her battered hull high above the level of the sea.

The *Douro*

In the spring of 1863 this fine steamer was captured at sea by the Federal cruisers, sent to a port of adjudication in the North, condemned and sold at auction, taken to the British Provinces (Halifax, I think) and there purchased, it was said, by the Confederate Government. At all events she was fitted out for the same service and in a few weeks reappeared at Nassau, where I saw her as a Confederate steamer under the Confederate flag. On the night of the 11th of October, 1863, the *Douro* attempted to run the blockade at New Inlet, loaded with a valuable cargo of 550 bales of cotton, 279 boxes of tobacco, 20 tierces of tobacco, and a quantity of turpentine and rosin, belonging to the Confederate Government. At 8.30 of the same night she eluded the Federal fleet and was running up the beach towards Masonboro in two and one-half fathoms of water, when she was pursued by the cruiser *Nansemond*, which tried to get between the *Douro* and the beach, but failed because of shoal water. Had the *Douro* kept on her course she would have escaped, but, taking a panic, she reversed her course, and headed back for the bar at New Inlet, was then intercepted by the *Nansemond* and run ashore, instead of facing the gun fire of the fleet with a chance of getting under Fort Fisher's protection. The captain and most of the crew escaped in the *Douro's* boats, but five, remaining on board, were captured by the cruiser *Nansemond*. It was said at the time that this fine ship (a propeller) was owned in Wilmington and that her cargo was for the Confederate Government. She now lies just above the *Hebe* between Fort Fisher and Masonboro Inlet.

Two of the finest blockade runners, sister ships, called the *Don* and the *Dee*, met at last with disaster. The *Don*, after running the gauntlet some ten or twelve times, was captured at sea. She had been commanded from her first voyage to the one before the last by Captain Roberts, so-called, really Captain Hobart, of the Royal British Navy, who later became Hobart Pasha, admiral in chief of the Turkish Navy. He was a son of the Earl of Buckinghamshire. The *Dee* was commanded for three successful voyages by Capt. George H. Bier, formerly a Lieutenant in the U.S. Navy. At 8 o'clock a.m. February 6, 1864, the *U.S.S. Cambridge* on the blockade off New Inlet discovered the *Dee* from Hamilton, Bermuda, loaded with pig lead, bacon, and military stores, bound for Wilmington, ashore and on fire about a mile to the southward of Masonboro Inlet.

The *Cambridge* at once boarded the stranded vessel and attempted to salve her, but the fire was too hot and the ship too deeply embedded in the sand to haul her off into deep water. She was accordingly bombarded and abandoned. The *Dee's* crew escaped to the shore, with the exception of seven men, who fell into the hands of the Federals. It is not known whether the *Dee* ran ashore from accident or design.

Steamer *Nutfield*

I learn from official reports that after Captain Roe of the *U.S.S. Sassacus* had practically destroyed the *Wild Dayrell* by gun fire he stood out to sea and regained his position in the outer line of cruisers, known as the Bermuda line or track, and that at daylight of the 4th of February, 1864, he discovered a blockade runner to the northward, which proved to be the fine

new iron steamer *Nutfield* of 750 tons (unusually large size), from Bermuda bound for Wilmington. The *Sassacus*, being the faster ship, increased her speed to thirteen knots, and at noon succeeded in getting in range of the *Nutfield* with her 100-pounder rifle guns, which did such execution that the hard pressed *Nutfield* changed her course, heading for the land, and ran ashore at New River

*The **Nutfield** was abandoned so fast that boarding Federals found the mess table still set.*

Inlet. The *Nutfield's* crew set her on fire and fled precipitately in their boats for the beach. One of the *Nutfield's* boats capsized in the surf and the Federals tried to rescue the crew but only succeeded in saving the purser, the others being supposedly drowned. Efforts were made by the *Sassacus* for two days to haul off the *Nutfield*, which was a very valuable prize, being loaded with an assorted cargo of merchandise, drugs, munitions of war, Enfield rifles, a battery of eight very valuable Whitworth guns, and a quantity of pig lead; the battery and the lead were thrown overboard during the chase. The *Nutfield* had escaped from the blockading fleet at New Inlet the night before and was off New River intending to try the Cape Fear the following night, but most unfortunately fell in with the *Sassacus*, a fast cruiser, during the day. A large part of her valuable cargo was taken out of her by the Federals.

The *Banshee*'s Narrow Escape*

Mr. Thomas E. Taylor was agent for the blockade runner *Banshee*, and I quote his narrative: "One very dark night (I think it was either on the fourth or fifth trip) we made the land about twelve miles above Fort Fisher, and were creeping quietly down as usual, when all at once we made a cruiser out, lying on our port bow, and slowly moving about 200 yards from the shore. It was a question of going inside or outside her; if we went outside she was certain to see us, and would chase us into the very jaws of the fleet. As we had very little steam up we chose the former alternative, hoping to pass unobserved between the cruiser and the shore, aided by the dark background of the latter. It was an exciting moment; we got almost abreast of her, as we thought, unobserved, and success seemed within our grasp, till we saw her move in toward us and heard her hail as we came on, 'Stop that steamer or I will sink you!'

"Old Steele growled out that we hadn't time to stop, and shouted down the engine-room tube to Erskine to pile on the coal, as concealment was no longer any use. Our friend, which we afterwards found out was the *Niphon*, opened fire as fast as she could and sheered close into us, so close that her boarders were called away twice, and a slanging match went on between us, like that sometimes to be heard between two penny steamboat captains on the Thames. She closed the dispute by shooting away our foremast, exploding a shell in our bunkers, and, when we began to leave her astern, by treating us to grape and canister. It was a miracle that no one was killed, but the crew were all lying flat on the deck, except the steersman; and at one time I fear he did the same, for as Pilot Burroughs suddenly cried, 'My God, Mr. Taylor, look there!' I saw our boat heading right into the surf, so, jumping from the bridge, I ran aft and found the helmsman on his stomach. I rushed at the wheel and got two or three spokes out of it, which hauled her head off land, but it was a close shave.

"Two miles farther we picked up another cruiser, which tried to treat us in a similar manner, but as we had plenty of steam we soon left her. A little farther we came across a large side-wheel boat, which tried to run us down, missing us only by a few yeards; after that we were unmolested and arrived in safe, warmly congratulated by Lamb, who thought from the violent cannonade that we must certainly be sunk.

---

*The *Banshee* and a few other blockade runners mentioned in this book as escaping capture were later either captured or stranded.

"Not more than one man out of a hundred would have brought a boat through as Steele did that night—the other ninety-nine would have run her ashore."

The *Venus*

The official report of Lieutenant Lamson, U.S. steamer *Nansemond*, off New Inlet, October 21, 1863, says, "I have the honor to report the capture and entire destruction of the blockade runner *Venus*, from Nassau to Wilmington with a cargo of lead, drugs, dry goods, bacon, and coffee.

"This morning at 12.30 she attempted to run the blockade, but was discovered by this vessel, and after a short chase overhauled. When abeam, I opened fire on her, one shot striking her foremast, another exploding in her wardroom, a third passing through forward and killing one man, and a fourth, striking under the guard near the water line, knocked in an iron plate, causing her to make water fast. She was run ashore. We boarded her at once, capturing her captain and twenty-two of her officers and crew. The *U.S.S. Niphon*, Acting Master J. B. Breck commanding, which was lying near where she went ashore, came immediately to my assistance. I ran a 9-inch hawser to the *Venus*, and Captain Breck sent a 7-inch hawser to the *Nansemond's* bow, but all our efforts were unavailing, as the tide had turned ebb and she was going at least 14 knots an hour when she went ashore. Finding it impossible to move her, I ordered her to be set on fire, which was done in three places by Acting Ensigns Porter and Henderson, of this vessel. Our boats were for some time exposed to a sharp fire of musketry from the beach, and the vessel was within range of one of the batteries. We had just commenced shelling her machinery when another vessel was seen off shore, and by the light of the burning steamer I was able to give her one shot and started in pursuit, but it was so cloudy and hazy that we lost sight of her almost immediately. I ran east at the rate of fourteen knots till 7 o'clock, but did not get sight of her again, and ran back, making the land on the northward.

"In the meantime, Captain Breck, with the assistance of the *Iron Age*, Lieut. Commander Stone, had completed the destruction of the *Venus*, her boilers having been blown up and her hull riddled with shell.

"I have to express my thanks to Captain Breck for the prompt assistance rendered me by sending his boats to assist in carrying my heavy hawser to the *Nansemond's* bows. His boats then reported to Acting Ensign

J. H. Porter, who was in charge of the *Venus*. The fire forward not burning well as it was expected, he sent a boat on board in the morning and rekindled it."

The *Venus* was 265 feet long and 1,000 tons measurement, and is represented by her captain and officers to have been one of the finest and fastest vessels engaged in running the blockade. She had the finest engines of any vessel in this trade and was sheathed completely over with iron. She drew eight feet of water, and when bound out last, crossed the bar at low water with over 600 bales of cotton on board. The wrecks of the *Hebe*, *Douro*, and *Venus* are within a short distance of each other.

A private notebook was found by the Federal boarding party in the effects of the captain of the *Venus*, in which a list of blockade runners engaged in the year 1863 was entered as follows, a total of 75 steamers, of which 34 were captured or destroyed, but this list was not complete, as a hundred at least were engaged during that period.

Vessels Engaged in Running the Blockade in 1863.
(Those marked C had been captured or destroyed.)

Nina (C)
Gladiator
Leopard (C)
Hebe (C)
Antonica
Venus (C)
Thistle (C)
Juno (C)
Douro (C)
Princess Royal (C)
Calypso (C)
Cronstadt (C)
Granite City (C)
Phantom (C)
Flora
Lord Clyde
Ruby (C)
Dolphin
Eagle (C)
Hansa
Havelock

Ella
Douglas
Spaulding (C)
Annie Childs (C)
Mary Ann
Wave Queen (C)
Mail (C)
Giraffe (C)
Spunkie
Cornubia (C)
Jupiter
Nicolai I (C)
Gibraltar
St. John (C)
Boston
Hero*
Juno II
Gertrude (C)
Scotia
Britannia (C)
Flora II
Emma (C)

Herald
Georgiana (C)
Elizabeth (C)
J. P. Hughes
R. E. Lee
Banshee
Beauregard
Alice (Mobile)
Sumter
Aries (St. Thomas) (C)
Corsica
Neptune (C)
Bendigo
Norseman (C)
Diamond
Merrimac (C)
Margaret and Jessie
Kate (C)
Don
Orion

Pet
Siriens (Sirius?)
Charleston
Atlantic
Rouen
EugÈnie
Hero II
Cuba (Mobile) (C)
Fanny
Raccoon
Stonewall Jackson
Arabian (C)

Total, 75; captured and destroyed, 34.

*Returned to England.

The *Hebe*

Between the 15th of August and the 21st of October, 1863, the Federal fleet known as the "North American Blockading Squadron" drove ashore five blockade runners between New Inlet and Masonboro—the *Arabian* inside the bar of New Inlet, which became an obstruction to our ships trying to pass her; the beautiful steamer *Hebe* near Masonboro Inlet, the *Phantom*, the *Douro*, and the *Venus* near each other off Masonboro Sound.

As her classical name implies, the *Hebe* was a fine example of marine architecture. She was loaded with a full cargo of drugs, coffee, clothing, and provisions, and although she was a fast ship of 14 knots, she seems to have made a bad landfall on the morning of the 18th of August, 1863, and while she was heading for New Inlet, distant about eight miles, she was intercepted by the Federal gunboat *Niphon*, when she up helm and ran ashore, the crew escaping in boats.

When the Federals attempted to haul the *Hebe* off the beach after she had run ashore, they met with formidable resistance by the Confederates. Owing to a heavy sea the *Niphon's* boat was driven ashore and the Federals were attacked by a troop of Confederate cavalry and all of them were captured. A Confederate force of riflemen, supported by a battery of Whitworth guns, also attacked the cruiser *Niphon* from the shore and drove the blockader away from the *Hebe*, but not before the Confederates

Lt. William B. Cushing,
U.S. Navy

had destroyed another Federal boat load of the enemy which attempted to land. The *Niphon* and the *Shokokon*, the latter under the command of the celebrated Lieut. W.B. Cushing, then bombarded the *Hebe* and set her on fire.

On August 24, 1863, General Whiting, in command of the Confederate forces at Wilmington headquarters, sent to the Secretary of War, Mr. Seddon, the following account of the *Hebe* disaster:

"Headquarters,
"*Wilmington, August 24, 1863.*

"Sir:

Yesterday the enemy took a fancy to destroy what remained of the wreck of the *Hebe,* a Crenshaw steamer run ashore some days ago, and from which a company of the garrison of Fort Fisher was engaged in saving property. The steam frigate *Minnesota* and five other gunboats approached the beach, and, under a terrific fire, attempted to land, but were gallantly repulsed by Captain Munn, with a Whitworth and two small rifle guns of short range. The site was about nine miles from Fisher, on the narrow and low beach between the sounds and the ocean, and completely under the fire of the enormous batteries of the enemy. A portion of the squadron, steaming farther up the beach, effected a landing some two miles off in largely superior force, and came down upon Captain Munn, still gallantly fighting his little guns against the *Minnesota,* they being moved by hand, and, having fired his last round, the Whitworths disabled, one gunner killed, a lieutenant and four men wounded, Captain Munn and his small party were compelled to fall back under a heavy enfilade fire toward Fort Fisher, with the loss of his guns.

A British-made Whitworth cannon

"This took place about nine miles from Fort Fisher and about the same distance from the city. The narrow beach, separated from the mainland by the sounds, gives every facility to the enemy, and secures them from us who are without boats or means of getting at them. The Fiftieth (North Carolina) Regiment—the only one I have—was off at a distance, called by a landing made by the enemy at Topsail, in which they burned, the night before, a schooner, a salt work, and took two artillerymen prisoners.

"These little affairs, however, are only mentioned in illustration. This is the first time they have landed; but what they have done once they can do again and doubtless will. There is no day scarcely until the winter gales set in but what they could put 5,000 men on the beach; they can get them from

New Berne and Beaufort before I could know it. I only say if they do they can get either Fort Fisher or the towns, as they elect, if they set about it at once.

"The efforts of the enemy to stop our steamers are increasing. Their force is largely increased. I have met with a serious and heavy loss in that Whitworth, a gun that in the hands of the indefatigable Lamb has saved dozens of vessels and millions of money to the Confederate States. I beg that a couple of the Whitworth guns originally saved by him from the *Modern Greece* may be sent here at once. Their long range, five or six miles, makes them most suitable for a seaboard position. Could I get them with horses we could save many a vessel that will now be lost to us. But chiefly in this letter I beg of you, if you concur in my views, to lay the matter of the necessity of increasing the force here before the President.

> "Very respectfully,
> "W.H.C. Whiting,
> "*Major General.*

"Hon. James A. Seddon,
"*Secretary War, Richmond.*"

A Port of Refuge

The natural advantages of Wilmington at the time of the War between the States made it an ideal port for blockade runners, there being two entrances to the river—New Inlet on the north and Western or Main Bar on the south of Cape Fear.

The slope of our beach is very gradual to deep water. The soundings along the coast are regular, and the floor of the ocean is remarkably even. A steamer hard pressed by the enemy could run along the outer edge of the breakers without great risk of grounding; the pursuer, being usually of deeper draft, was obliged to keep farther off shore.

The *Lilian*

The Confederate steamer *Lilian*, of which I was then purser, was chased for nearly a hundred miles from Cape Lookout by the U.S. steamer *Shenandoah*, which sailed a parallel course within half a mile of her and forced the *Lilian* at times into the breakers. This was probably the narrowest escape ever made by a blockade runner in a chase. The *Shenandoah* began firing her broadside guns at three o'clock in the afternoon, her gunners and

The **U.S.S. Shenandoah,** *on station in China after the Civil War.*

the commanding officers of the batteries being distinctly visible to the *Lilian's* crew. A heavy sea was running, which deflected the aim of the man-of-war, and this alone saved the *Lilian* from destruction. A furious bombardment by the *Shenandoah*, aggravated by the display of the *Lilian's* Confederate flag, was continued until nightfall, when, by a clever ruse, the *Lilian*, guided by the flash of her pursuer's guns, stopped for a few minutes; then, putting her helm hard over, ran across the wake of the warship straight out to sea, and, on the following morning, passed the fleet off Fort Fisher in such a crippled condition that several weeks were spent in Wilmington for repairs.

The *Lynx* and Her Pilot

He is now the Rev. James William Craig,* Methodist preacher, but I like to think of him as Jim Billy, the Cape Fear pilot of war times, on the bridge of the swift Confederate blockade runner *Lynx*, commanded by the intrepid Captain Reed, as she races through the blackness of night on her course west nor'west, straight and true for the Federal fleet off New Inlet, in utter silence, the salt spray of the sea smiting the faces of the watches as they gaze ahead for the first sign of imminent danger.

---

*Mr. Craig has since died.

Soon there is added to the incessant noise of wind and waves the ominous roar of the breakers, as the surf complains to the shore, and the deep sea lead gives warning of shoaling water. "Half-speed" is muttered through the speaking tube; a hurried parley; a recognized landfall, for Reed is a fine navigator, and "Are you ready to take her, Pilot?" "Ready, sir," comes from Jim Billy in the darkness. Then the whispered orders through the tube: "Slow down," as there looms ahead the first of the dread monsters of destruction; "Starboard," "Steady." And the little ship glides past like a phantom, unseen as yet. Then "Port," "Port," "Hard a'port," in quick succession, as she almost touches the second cruiser. She is now in the thick of the blockading squadron; and suddenly, out of the darkness, close aboard, comes the hoarse hail, "Heave to, or I'll sink you," followed by a blinding glare of rockets and the roar of heavy guns. The devoted little Confederate is now naked to her enemies, as the glare of rockets and Drummond lights from many men-of-war illuminate the chase. Under a pitiless hail of shot and shell from every quarter, she bounds forward full speed ahead, every joint and rivet straining, while Jim Billy dodges her in and out through a maze of smoke and flame and bursting shells. The range of Fort Fisher's guns is yet a mile away. Will she make it? Onward speeds the little ship, for neither Reed nor Jim Billy has a thought of surrender. A shell explodes above them, smashing the wheelhouse; another shell tears away the starboard paddle box; and, as she flies like lightning past the nearest cruiser, a sullen roar from Colonel Lamb's artillery warns her pursuers that they have reached their limitations, and in a few minutes the gallant little ship crosses the bar and anchors under the Confederate guns. The captain and his trusty pilot shake hands and go below, "to take the oath," as Reed described it—for the strain must be relaxed by sleep or stimulation. "A close shave, Jim," was all the captain said. "It was, sir, for a fact," was the equally laconic answer.

The *Ranger* and the *Vesta*

These two fine ships were stranded on our coast upon their first voyage and as I had no personal knowledge of either of them, I have copied in full the Federal official reports, and a letter dated Wilmington, N.C., January 27, 1864, by Lieutenant Gift of the Confederate Navy, who was in command of the *Ranger*.

"U.S. Flagship *Minnesota*,
"Off Lockwood's Folly Inlet,
"January 11, 1864.

"Sir:

At daylight this morning a steamer was seen beached and burning one mile west of this inlet. Mr. O'Connor, from this ship, boarded her with the loss of one man, shot under the fire from the enemy's sharp shooters occupying rifle pits on the sand hills, which were high and near, and got her log book, from which it appears that she is the *Ranger;* that she left Newcastle [England] November 11, 1863, for Bermuda, where, after touching at Teneriffe, she arrived on the 8th of December; that she sailed from Bermuda January 6, 1864, made our coast January 10, about five miles northeast of Murrell's Inlet, and landed her passengers. The next morning at daylight, intercepted by this ship, the *Daylight, Governor Buckingham,* and *Aries*, in her approach to Western Bar, she was beached and fired by her crew, as above mentioned. The attempts of the *Governor Buckingham*, aided by the *Daylight* and *Aries*, to extinguish the fire and haul the *Ranger* off were frustrated by the enemy's sharp-shooters, whose fire completely commanded her decks. This ship, drawing about twenty-four feet, was taken in four and one-half fathoms of water in front of the wreck, and the other vessels stationed to cross fire on the riflemen on the sand hills opened a deliberate fire with a view to dislodge the enemy and allow an attempt to haul off the *Ranger* at high water at night. Meanwhile, the *Ranger* was burning freely forward and the commanding officers of the *Governor Buckingham* and *Daylight*, who had a good view of her situation, thinking

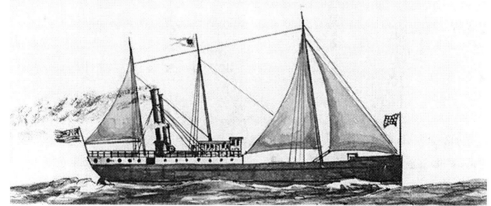

The U.S.S. Daylight *was the first Union vessel to blockade the Cape Fear.*

that it was not practicable to get her off, she was also fired into, which, as her hatches were closed, had the effect of letting the air in, when the fire burned freely aft and doubtless burned the *Ranger* out completely. Meanwhile, black smoke was rising in the direction of Shallotte Inlet, and the *Aries*, withdrawn last night from her station there, was ordered to chase. She soon returned, and Acting Volunteer Lieutenant Devens reported a fine - looking double - propeller blockade runner, resembling the *Ceres*, beached and on fire between Tubb's and Little River Inlets, and that the enemy's sharpshooters prevented his boats from boarding her. This was probably the same steamer that was chased the previous evening by the *Quaker City, Tuscarora,* and *Keystone State,* and escaping from them made the western shore, where, communicating and learning of the presence of the blockaders in force, and perhaps being short of coal, was beached by her crew and fired rather than be captured.

"The Department will perceive that this is the twenty-second steamer lost by the rebels and the blockade runners attempting to violate the blockade of Wilmington within the last six months, an average of nearly one steamer every eight days. These losses must greatly lessen the means of the rebel authorities to export cotton, obtain supplies, and sustain their credit, and thus dispirit and weaken them very much.

"I have the honor to be, Sir,
"Very respectfully yours,
"S. P. Lee,
Acting Rear Admiral,
"Comdg. North Atlantic Blockading Squadron.

"Hon. Gideon Welles,
"Secretary of the Navy,
"Washington, D. C."

"U.S.S. Aries,
"Off Little River,
"January 12, 1864.

"Sir:
I would most respectfully report that the steamer stranded between Tubb's Inlet and Little River is the blockade runner *Vesta.* Boarded her this

a.m.; made a hawser fast to her, but on examining her found her whole starboard side opened and several of the plates split; took two anchors from her, which was all we could save.

"The *Vesta* was exactly like the *Ceres*.

"I left her a complete wreck, with five feet of water in her. Her boats lay on the beach badly stove.

"Very respectfully,
your obedient servant,
"Edward F. Devens,
"Acting Volunteer Lieutenant, Commanding."

"Wilmington, N.C.,
January 27, 1864.

"My Dear Sir:
In Bermuda I took command of a splendid merchant steamer, called the *Ranger*, for the passage to Wilmington. I had very heavy weather and no observation for the first three days out. On the fourth got sights which put me at noon eighty miles southeast from lightship off Frying Pan Shoals. I went ahead full speed in heavy sea to sight the light early in the night, but the Yankees had put it out, and fearing the drift of the Gulf, I determined to run inshore and anchor during the next day (10th instant) and ascertain my position accurately, which I did, and landed my passengers and baggage. On the morning of the 11th, at 12.25 a.m., I got underway and ran along the coast for the bar near Fort Caswell. When eight miles from the fort I made the *Minnesota* about one mile off, and whilst observing her motions the pilot (who had charge of the ship) suddenly sheered her inshore, and in an instant she was in the breakers. I made every effort to get her off, but unavailingly, so you see a couple of turns of a wheel in the hands of a timid man lost a fine ship and a valuable cargo. She was destroyed. I was loaded for Government.

"Your obedient servant,
"George W. Gift."

The **U.S.S. Quaker City.**

The *Spunkie*

Many blockade runners were given corresponding names, *Owl, Bat, Badger, Phantom, Lynx,* but none seemed to be more appropriate than that given to a little toy steamer from the Clyde named *Spunkie.* She was not fast but she managed to make several successful runs. When I saw her in Nassau I could scarcely believe that this little cockleshell of a boat had crossed the North Atlantic and had run through the blockading fleet. The commander of the Federal cruiser *Quaker City* reported to Admiral Lee February 13, 1864, that he had discovered the *Spunkie* ashore at daylight on the 9th on the beach short distance west of Fort Caswell, but he could not determine whether she was attempting to run in or run out. Two tugs belonging to the blockading fleet made repeated but ineffectual efforts to float the *Spunkie* and she still lies near Fort Caswell. As the *Spunkie* was loaded with blankets, shoes, and provisions for the Confederate soldiers, there is no doubt she was trying to come into the river by the Western Bar when she ran ashore.

The *Phantom*

This was a new Confederate steamer built abroad on the most approved lines for the Confederate Government. She was a handsome iron propeller of about 500 tons, camouflaged, as were all blockade runners, to decrease her visibility. The usual method was to paint the hull and smoke funnels a grayish green to correspond with the sea and sky and the coast-line sand dunes, which often made them invisible even at close range. There were two Federal cruisers most dreaded by the blockade runners beacuse of their great speed: the *Connecticut* and the *Fort Jackson*. The former made many prizes. At daylight, the morning of September 23, 1863, when about fifty miles east by north of New Inlet, the *Phantom* was discovered by the *Connecticut* standing to the eastward. The *Phantom* was bound from Bermuda for Wilmington with a very valuable cargo of Confederate arms, medicine, and general stores. She had evidently made a very bad landfall too far to the northward and eastward at daylight and was running away from the land until darkness would help her into Cape Fear River, when she would face the fleet again. But the *Connecticut* gave chase at her top speed and after four hours' vain effort to escape, the *Phantom* suddenly hauled in and ran ashore near Rich Inlet, where she still lies. The crew escaped in their own boats, after setting the *Phantom* on fire. The Federals attempted to put out the fire and salve the *Phantom*, but failed to do so.

The U.S.S. Connecticut.

The *Dare*

This steamer was built abroad in 1863 for the Confederate Government. At daybreak on the morning of the 7th of January, 1864, the cruiser *Montgomery* saw the *Dare* with Confederate colors flying near Lockwood's Folly, heading for Cape Fear. The *Montgomery* and her consort the *Aries* gave chase, the latter heading off the *Dare*, which endeavored to escape, but being in range of the guns of both pursuers for about four hours, she headed for the beach, and was stranded at 12.30 p.m. a little to the northward of North Inlet, near Georgetown, S.C. The weather was very stormy and the surf very high so that one of the Federal boats, in attempting to board the *Dare*, was capsized and her crew made prisoners by the Confederates behind the sand dunes. Other Federal boats reached the stranded vessel and set her on fire.

The officers and crew of the *Dare* escaped to the shore.

The *Bendigo*

In 1863, when the demand for suitable merchant steamers to run the Wilmington blockade could not be met, even at enormous prices, the eager buyers began to bid on the Clyde River steamers. Some of extraordinary speed but of frail construction were lost on the long and often tempestous voyage across the Atlantic via Madeira and Bermuda, while others succeeded in passing the blockade with almost the regularity of mail boats. Of such was the *Bendigo*, previously named the *Milly*. Her description was as follows: Topsail yard schooner *Bendigo*; steamship of Liverpool, late *Milly*, 178 tons, built of iron, hull painted green, three portholes on either side fore and aft of paddle boxes. Elliptic stern, carriage and name on same painted white, bridge athwartships on top of paddle boxes; after funnel or smokestack, with steam pipe fore part of same; fire funnel or smoke stack with steam pipe fore part of same; draws eight feet six inches aft and eight feet forward.

I am putting this description (now obsolete) on record because it was a type of many other blockade runners in 1863-64.

The *Wilmington Journal* of January 11, 1864, described the stranding of the blockade runner *Bendigo* at Lockwood's Folly Inlet, from which it appears that the wreck of the blockade runner *Elizabeth* was mistaken by the *Bendigo* for a Federal cruiser, and in trying to run between the wreck and the beach the *Bendigo* was stranded. The *Bendigo* was discovered at 11 a.m.

Wreck of the **U.S.S. Iron Age** *in Lockwood Folly, 2004.*

January 4, 1864, by Acting Rear Admiral S. P. Lee on his flagship *Fahkee*, who attempted with the assistance of the *Fort Jackson, Iron Age, Montgomery*, and *Daylight* to haul off the *Bendigo*, in which they failed because the Confederate batteries on shore drove them off with the loss of the *Iron Age*, which got aground and blew up. The *Bendigo* was set on fire and abandoned and her hull may be still visible at Lockwood's Folly Bar.

The *Antonica*

This Confederate blockade runner I remember as a fine ship and very successful. She was of the old American type of passenger and mail boat, 516 tons, known previously as the *Herald*. So regular and reliable in her runs was she that I recall a remark of one of her officers that it was only necessary to start her engine, put her on her course for either Wilmington or Nassau, lash her wheel, and she would go in and out by herself.

She ran several times in and out of Charleston, where she was registered carrying 1,000 to 1,200 bales of cotton and some tobacco. She was commanded on her last voyage by Capt. W. F. Adair, who reported that on the night of the 19th of December, 1863, the *Antonica* made the land at Little River Inlet, the dividing line between North Carolina and South Carolina, and stood to the eastward of Lockwood's Folly Inlet and waited until the moon set at 2.30 a.m., when he attempted to run the blockade at Cape Fear Bar, but in trying to pass the blockader *Governor Buckingham* was forced ashore on Frying Pan Shoals, and he and his crew, twenty-six all told, were captured while making for the beach in their own boats.

The *Antonica* was loaded and bound for Wilmington with a very valuable cargo of war supplies when she was lost. The wreck still remains on Frying Pan Shoals.

I recall an interesting episode with reference to the *Antonica* which nearly caused a rupture between the British and Federal Governments while I was with my ship in the British port of Nassau. The incident was referred to by the late Capt. Michael Usina of Savannah in his most interesting address many years ago before the Confederate Veterans, and I repeat it in his words:

"On one occasion I was awakened by the sound of cannon in the early morning at Nassau, and imagine my surprise to see a Confederate ship being fired at by a Federal man-of-war. The Confederate proved to be the *Antonica*, Captain Coxetter, who arrived off the port during the night, and, waiting for a pilot and daylight, found when daylight did appear that an enemy's ship was between him and the bar. There was nothing left for him to do but run the gauntlet and take his fire, which he did in good shape, some of the shot actually falling into the harbor. The Federal ship was commanded by Commodore Wilkes, who became widely known from taking Mason and Slidell prisoners. After the chase was over Wilkes anchored his ship, and when the Governor sent to tell him that he must not remain at anchor there he said: 'Tell the Governor, etc., etc., he would anchor where he pleased.' The military authorities sent their artillery across to Hog Island, near where he

Captain Michael Usina

was anchored, and we Confederates thought the fun was about to begin. But Wilkes remained just long enough to communicate with the consul and get what information he wanted, and left."

The *Florie* and the *Badger*

These two fine boats were well known to me. The former was named after Mrs. J. G. Wright, of Wilmington, the beautiful daughter of Capt. John N. Maffitt, who commanded my ship the *Lilian*, a sister boat.

The *Florie* was owned by the State of Georgia and by some of its prominent citizens, Gov. Joseph Brown, Col. C.A.L. Lamar, and others. She made several successful runs to Wilmington, but her end is clouded in mystery. There is no record of her fate except a report by some "intelligent contrabands" to the Federal fleet that she was sunk inside the bar in Cape Fear River; whether by accident or by shell fire I am unable to ascertain. It was said that the *Badger*, sister ship to the *Lynx*, came to her end the same way after making several runs through the fleet.

The following order of the Confederate Secretary of the Navy to Capt. John N. Maffitt, who was then in command of the *Owl*, will explain why so many valuable ships were run ashore rather than surrendered into the hands of the Federals:

The blockade-runner Badger.

Order of the Secretary of the Navy to Commander Maffitt, C.S. Navy, repeating telegram of instructions regarding the command of the blockade runner *Owl.*

"Confederate States of America,
"Navy Department, Richmond,
"September 19, 1864.

"Sir:

The following telegram was this day sent to you:

"It is of the first importance that our steamers should not fall into the enemy's hands. Apart from the specific loss sustained by the country in the capture of blockade runners, these vessels, lightly armed, now constitute the fleetest and most efficient part of his blockading force off Wilmington.

"As commanding officer of the *Owl* you will please devise and adopt thorough and efficient means for saving all hands and destroying the vessel and cargo whenever these measures may become necessary to prevent capture. Upon your firmness and ability the Department relies for the execution of this important trust. In view of this order, no passenger will, as a general rule, be carried. Such exceptions to this rule as the public interests may render necessary, embracing those who may be sent by the Government, will receive special permits from this Department.

"Assistant Paymaster Tredwell has been instructed to pay over to you, taking your receipt for the same, 5,000 pounds in sterling bills. You will please keep an accurate account with vouchers in duplicate of all your expenditures, one set of which you will submit to Mr. W.H. Peters, our special agent at Wilmington, upon each round trip you may make.

"I am respectfully your obedient servant,
"S. R. Mallory,
"*Secretary of the Navy.*

"Commander John N. Maffitt, *C.S. Navy,*
"Care W. H. Peters, Esq.,
"Wilmington, N. C."

The *Cape Fear*

A notable blockade runner called the *Virginia* was bought by the Confederate Government during the war and renamed the *Cape Fear.* She was put under the command of Captain Guthrie, a Cape Fear pilot of recognized ability, who was succeeded by an English gentleman, a fine sailor, Captain Wise, who cast his lot with our people and ran the *Cape Fear* up and down the river for several years as a Confederate transport. She was destroyed in the river when the Federals captured Fort Fisher. Captain Wise married a Miss Flora McCaleb, of Wilmington, and for years after the war conducted a lumberyard here. He was a most courteous, attractive gentleman, generally respected in the community. He died here many years ago.

The *North Heath*

During the third year of the War between the States, I was appointed at the age of seventeen years purser of the blockade-running steamer *North Heath*, under command of Captain Burroughs, who had successfully run the blockade twelve times in charge of the Confederate steamer *Cornubia*, later named *Lady Davis*, after the wife of the President. I believe that under God, Captain Burroughs, by his fine qualities as a cool and capable seaman, saved this ship from foundering at sea when we ran into a hurricane shortly after our departure from St. George, Bermuda, bound for Wilmington. For two days and nights we were in imminent danger of our lives—tossed upon a raging sea, every man of our crew of 48 except those at the wheel was lashed to the vessel, while we bailed with buckets and the use of hand pumps the flooded fireroom of our sinking vessel. For an entire night she wallowed like a log in a trough of mountainous waves, which broke over us

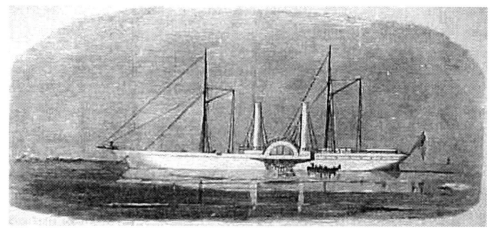

The blockade-runner **Lady Davis,** *formerly the* **Cornubia.**

in ever-increasing fury. I can never forget this frightful scene. It seems photographed upon my memory in all its fearsome details.

The water had risen in our hold until every one of our fourteen furnaces was extinguished. There was no steam to run our donkey boilers and steam-power pumps. Lashed to one another, in the blackness of darkness, relieved only by the intermittent flashes of lightning which illuminated the giant waves towering around us and threatening to overwhelm and sink the laboring, quivering fabric, we held on in despair until morning, when we began to gain on the leaks until our steam pumps could be used in relieving the boiler room, and our brave captain got the ship under control. Then we succeeded in putting her about and headed back to Bermuda.

The strain of this exposure resulted in an attack of fever, which confined me to bed for a long time on shore, and Captain Burroughs reluctantly left me behind when the ship was ready for sea. After we repaired our badly damaged hull and machinery, the *North Heath* proceeded again toward Wilmington, passing the blockading fleet safely. When she was about to load cotton for the outward voyage, the Federal expedition against Fort Fisher arrived off Cape Fear and presented such a formidable appearance that the Confederate Government seized the *North Heath*, loaded her with stone and sank her at a point below Sunset Park where the river channel is narrow, as an obstruction to the Federal fleet which subsequently captured Wilmington. For many years after she was an obstruction to peaceful commerce, but the wreck was finally removed by the River and Harbor Improvement Engineers.

The *Kate*

There were two blockade runners named *Kate*, but they were quite different as to origin and enterprise. The first one of that name was an American-built steamer, previously in the coast trade. She was commanded by Capt. Thomas J. Lockwood, and it was this vessel that brought to Wilmington on the 6th of August, 1862, the fearful plague of yellow fever, which raged for ten weeks and carried off 446 of our people. After several successful voyages she ran ashore above Fiddler's Dreen, near Southport, and went to pieces.

About twenty years ago I related in Justice Clark's *North Carolina Regimental Histories*, published in five volumes, 1901, an incident in the career of this steamer *Kate* which may be worth repeating:

On one occasion in the *Kate* Lockwood had run inside the line of blockaders at the Main Bar some distance up the beach, and suddenly took the ground while jammed between an anchored man-of-war and the breakers. The blockader did not see him, although so near that no one on board the *Kate* was permitted to speak above a whisper. The tide was near the last of the ebb and there were only a few hours of darkness in which to work. George C. McDougal, chief engineer and Captain Lockwood's brother-in-law, always ready for an emergency, had promptly loaded the safety valve down with a bag of iron castings to prevent any noise from escaping steam, and when it became absolutely necessary the steam was blown off very gently under the water. The boats were lowered noiselessly and several passengers and a lot of valuables landed in the surf on the lee side of the vessel, with orders to proceed to Fort Caswell in the distance. At first it seemed impossible to save the ship, as any noise from her paddles would inevitably have led to her destruction by the blockaders, which were seen plainly only a cable's length from the *Kate's* perilous position. Lockwood held a consultation with his trusted engineer, and decided to open the gangway and quietly slide overboard a lot of lead wire in heavy coils, which was part of the inward cargo, and which was intended to be cut into bullets by the Confederate Government. This served to lighten the ship and also as an effectual bulkhead which prevented the vessel from working higher up on the beach when the tide turned, and the discharge went on for some time without apparent effect; but the rising tide soon after began to bump the bilges of the vessel against the sand bank inside. Lockwood proposed an attempt to back clear or to beach her at once, but the "Boss," as

McDougal was called, calmly showed him that unless they were sure of floating clear on the first attempt they would never be permitted to make a second trial, as the paddles would surely betray them to the fleet. Another fifteen minutes that seemed an hour of suspense, and the captain again urged immediate action, but the imperturbable engineer said: "Wait a little longer, Oakie; she is rising every minute; let us be sure of getting off before we make the effort." Meantime the bumping increased, and at last, with everything in readiness and a full head of steam, the engines were reversed full speed, and the *Kate* quickly afloat and responding to the wheel, gallantly passed the blockading fleet in the gray dawn and shortly afterwards anchored under the guns of Fort Caswell. She had hardly swung to the anchor before she was seen by the disappointed blockaders, who sent shell after shell flying after her, bursting in such uncomfortable proximity, that the *Kate* was moved up to Mrs. Stuart's wharf at Smithville, where the shell and solid shot still followed her, many passing in a line more than a thousand yards beyond the wharf. With the aid of a good glass a man could be seen in the foretop of the Federal flagship with a flag in his hand, which he waved to right or left as he saw the effect of the firing; this enabled the gunners to better their aim until the shells struck just astern of the *Kate* or passed in a line ahead of the vessel. On a closer approach of the fleet they were driven off by Fort Caswell's heaviest guns. The *Kate* and her crew were in great peril on this occasion, owing to the fact that there were a thousand barrels of gunpowder on board for the Confederacy, making the risk from the shells extremely dangerous. Mr. McDougal said to me on this occasion that when the Yankees began shelling them at Fort Caswell a detachment of soldiers was being embarked for Wilmington on the Confederate transport *James T. Petteway*, and that when the first shell struck the beach near the *Petteway*, the whole company broke ranks and ran like rabbits to the fort again.

Some time ago the *Wilmington Daily Review* published an account of the recovery of a large lot of wire from the bottom of the sea near Fort Caswell. This was doubtless part of the *Kate's* cargo thrown overboard as described.

The Second *Kate*

The second *Kate* was a new iron steamer, double-screw propeller, 344 tons, English built, commanded by Captain Stubbs. She had made a successful run into Charleston with a valuable cargo, and was also successful in running out again with 700 bales of cotton, which she landed in Nassau.

She had loaded a second inward cargo at Nassau and sailed for Charleston, but, failing to elude the blockaders, she ran for Wilmington and on July 12, 1863, at 4.55 o'clock a.m., was making for New Inlet close ahead when she was intercepted by the Federal blockader *Penobscot*, which opened a heavy fire on her and drove her ashore on the south end of Smith's Island, where her wrecked hull still remains. The Federals attempted to haul the *Kate* off into deep water, but were prevented by the Confederates on shore, who drove them away. With the exception of two of her crew who remained and were captured, the officers and men of the *Kate* escaped to the shore.

The *Night Hawk*

It is not surprising that the Federal blockading fleet so often failed to refloat blockade runners after they were stranded on the beach, because the runners always timed their attempt to pass the fleet at high tide, the depth of water on the bar being only 10 to 12 feet and the channel beset with shoals and obstructions, so that before the Federals could prepare for hauling off these vessels and thereby secure for themselves large sums of prize money, the tide would have fallen, leaving the stranded ships more firmly embedded in the sand, and when in daylight another high tide would come the Federals had to deal with the Confederate guns, which kept them at a distance. There were, however, several instances which I recall of the rescue of stranded ships by the Confederates, notably that of the *Kate* and of the *Night Hawk*. The latter was a most spectacular, exciting affair, which I will relate in Mr. Thomas Taylor's words:

"It was on my second trip to Bermuda that one of the finest boats we ever possessed, called the *Night Hawk*, came out, and I concluded to run in with her. She was a new side-wheel steamer of some 600 tons gross, rigged as a fore-and-aft schooner, with two funnels, 220 feet long, 21 1/2 feet beam, and 11 feet in depth; a capital boat for the work, fast, strong, of light draught, and a splendid sea boat—a great merit in a blockade runner, which sometimes has to be forced in all weathers. The *Night Hawk's* career was a very eventful one, and she passed an unusually lively night off Fort Fisher on her first attempt.

"Soon after getting under way our troubles began. We ran ashore outside Hamilton, one of the harbors of Bermuda, and hung on a coral reef for a couple of hours. There loomed before us the dismal prospect of delay for repairs, or, still worse, the chance of springing a leak and experiencing such difficulties and dangers as we had undergone on the *Will-o'-the-Wisp*, but fortunately we came off without damage and were able to proceed on our voyage.

"Another anxiety now engrossed my mind: the captain was an entirely new hand, and nearly all the crew were green at the work; moreover, the Wilmington pilot was quite unknown to me, and I could see from the outset that he was very nervous and badly wanting in confidence. What would I not have given for our trusty pilot Tom Burriss! However, we had to make the best of it, as, owing to the demand, the supply of competent pilots was not nearly sufficient, and toward the close of the blockade the so-called pilots were no more than boatmen or men who had been trading in and out of Wilmington or Charleston in coasters.

"Notwithstanding my fears, all went well on the way across, and the *Night Hawk* proved to be everything that could be desired in speed and seaworthiness. We had sighted unusually few craft, and nothing eventful occurred until the third night. Soon after midnight we found ourselves uncomfortably near a large vessel. It was evident that we had been seen, as we heard them beating to quarters and were hailed. We promptly sheered off and went full speed ahead, greeted by a broadside which went across our stern. When we arrived within striking distance of Wilmington Bar, the pilot was anxious to go in by Smith's Inlet, but as he acknowledged that he knew very little about it, I concluded it was better to keep to the New Inlet passage, where, at all events, we should have the advantage of our good friend Lamb to protect us; and I felt that as I myself knew the place so well, this was the safest course to pursue. We were comparatively well through the fleet, although heavily fired at, and arrived near to the bar, passing close by two Northern launches which were lying almost upon it. Unfortunately, it was dead low water, and although I pressed the pilot to give our boat a turn around, keeping under way, and to wait awhile until the tide made, he was so demoralized by the firing we had gone through and the nearness of the launches, which were constantly throwing up rockets, that he insisted upon putting her at the bar, and, as I feared, we grounded on it forward and with the strong flood tide quickly broached to, broadside on to the northern breakers. We kept our engines going for some time, but to no purpose, as we found we were only being forced by the tide more on to the breakers. Therefore we stopped, and all at once found our friends, the two launches, close aboard; they had discovered we were ashore, and had made up their minds to attack us.

"At once all was in confusion; the pilot and signalman rushed to the dinghy, lowered it, and made good their escape; the captain lost his head and disappeared; and the crews of the launches, after firing several volleys, one of which slightly wounded me, rowed in to board us on each sponson. Just at this moment I suddenly recollected that our private dispatches, which ought to have been thrown overboard, were still in the starboard lifeboat. I rushed to it, but found the lanyard to which the sinking weight was attached was foul of one of the thwarts; I tugged and tugged, but to no purpose, so I sung out for a knife, which was handed to me by a fireman, and I cut the line and pitched the bag overboard as the Northerners jumped on board. Eighteen months afterwards that fireman accosted me in the Liverpool streets, saying, 'Mr. Taylor, do you remember my lending you a knife?' 'Of course I do,' I replied, giving him a tip at which he was mightily pleased. Poor fellow! he had been thirteen months in a Northern prison.

"When the Northerners jumped on board they were terribly excited. I don't know whether they expected resistance or not, but they acted more like maniacs than sane men, firing their revolvers and cutting right and left with their cutlasses. I stood in front of the men on the poop and said that we surrendered, but all the reply I received from the lieutenant commanding was, 'Oh, you surrender, do you?' accompanied by a string of the choicest Yankee oaths and sundry reflections upon my parentage; whereupon he fired his revolver twice point blank at me not two yards distant; it was a miracle he did not kill me, as I heard the bullets whiz past my head. This roused my wrath, and I expostulated in the strongest terms upon his firing on unarmed men; he then cooled down, giving me into charge of two of his men, one of whom speedily possessed himself of my binocular. Fortunately, as I had no guard to my watch, they didn't discover it, and I have it still.

"Finding they could not get the ship off, and afraid, I presume, of Lamb and his men coming to our rescue, the Federals commenced putting the captain (who had been discovered behind a boat!) and the crew into the boats; they then set the ship on fire fore and aft, and she soon began to blaze merrily. At this moment one of our firemen, an Irishman, sang out, 'Begorra, we shall all be in the air in a minute; the ship is full of gunpowder!' No sooner did the Northern sailors hear this than a panic seized them, and they rushed to their boats, threatening to leave their officers behind if they did not come along. The men who were holding me dropped me like a hot potato, and to my great delight jumped into their boat, and away they rowed as fast as they could, taking all our crew, with the exception of the second officer, one of the engineers, four seamen, and myself, as prisoners.

"We chuckled at our lucky escape, but we were not out of the woods yet, as we had only a boat half stove in in which to reach the shore through some three hundred yards of surf, and we were afraid at any moment that our enemies, finding there was no powder on board, might return. We made a feeble effort to put the fire out, but it had gained too much headway, and although I offered the men with me £50 apiece to stand by me and persevere, they were too demoralized and began to lower the shattered boat, swearing they would leave me behind if I didn't come with them. There was nothing for it but to go, yet the passage through the boiling surf seemed more dangerous to my mind than remaining on the burning ship. The blockaders immediately opened fire when they knew their own men had left the *Night Hawk* and that she was burning; and Lamb's great shells hurtling over our heads, and those from the blockading fleet bursting all around us, formed a weird picture. In spite of the hail of shot and shell and the dangers of the boiling surf, we reached the shore in safety, wet through, and glad I was, in my state of exhaustion from loss of blood and fatigue, to be welcomed by Lamb's orderly officer.

"The poor *Night Hawk* was now a sheet of flame, and I thought it was all up with her; and indeed it would have been had it not been for Lamb, who, calling for volunteers from his garrison, sent off two or three boat loads of men to her, and when I came down to the beach, after having my wound dressed and a short rest, I was delighted to find the fire had visibly decreased. I went on board, and after some hours of hard work the fire was extinguished. But what a wreck she was!

"Luckily, with the rising tide she had bumped over the bank, and was now lying on the main beach much more accessible and sheltered. Still it seemed an almost hopeless task to save her; but we were not going to be beaten without a try, so, having ascertained how she lay and the condition she was in, I resolved to have an attempt made to get her dry, and telegraphed to Wilmington for assistance.

"Our agent sent me down about three hundred negroes to assist in bailing and pumping, and I set them to work at once. As good luck would have it, my finest steamer, *Banshee No. 2*, which had just been sent out, ran in the next night. She was a great improvement on the first *Banshee*, having a sea speed of 15 and a half knots, which was considered very fast in those days; her length was 252 feet, beam 31 feet, depth 11 feet, her registered tonnage 439 tons, and her crew consisted of fifty-three in all. I at once requisitioned her for aid in the shape of engineers and men, so that now I had everything I could want in the way of hands. Our great difficulty was that the *Night Hawk's* anchors would not hold for us to get a fair haul at her.

"But here again I was to be in luck. For the very next night the *Condor*, commanded by poor Hewett, in attempting to run in stuck fast upon the bank over which we had bumped, not one hundred yards to windward of us, and broke in two. It is an ill wind that blows nobody good, and Hewett's mischance proved the saving of our ship. Now we had a hold for our chain cables by making them fast to the wreck, and were able gradually to haul her off by them a little during each tide, until on the seventh day we had her afloat in a gut between the bank and the shore, and at high water we steamed under our own steam gaily up the river to Wilmington.

"Considering the appliances we had and the circumstances under which we were working, the saving of that steamer was certainly a wonderful performance, as we were under fire almost the whole time. The Northerners, irritated, no doubt, by their failure to destroy the ship, used to shell us by day and send in boats by night; Lamb, however, put a stop to the latter annoyance by lending us a couple of companies to defend us, and one night, when our enemies rowed close up with the intention of boarding us, they were glad to sheer off with the loss of a lieutenant and several men. In spite of all the shot and shell by day and the repeated attacks by night, we triumphed in the end, and, after having the *Night Hawk* repaired at a huge cost and getting together a crew, I gave May, a friend of mine, command of her, and he ran her out successfully with a valuable cargo, which made her pay, notwithstanding all her bad luck and the amount spent upon her. Poor May! he was afterwards governor of Perth gaol, and is dead now—a high-toned, sensitive gentleman, mightily proud of his ship, lame duck as she was.

"When she was burning, our utmost efforts were of course directed toward keeping her engine room and boilers amidships intact, and confining the flames to both ends; in this we were successful, mainly owing to the fact of her having thwartship bunkers; but as regards the rest of the steamer she was a complete wreck; her sides were all corrugated with the heat, and her stern so twisted that her starboard quarter was some two feet higher than her port quarter, and not a particle of wood work was left unconsumed. Owing to the limited resources of Wilmington as regards repairs, I found it impossible to have this put right, so her sides were left as they were, and the new deck put on the slope I have described, and caulked with cotton, as no oakum was procurable. When completed she certainly was a queer looking craft, but as tight as a bottle and as seaworthy as ever, although I doubt if any Lloyd's surveyor would have passed her. But as a matter of fact she came across the Atlantic, deeply immersed with her coal supply, through some very bad weather, without damage, and was sold for a mere song, to be repaired and made into a passenger boat for service on the East Coast, where she ran for many years with success.

"It had been a hard week for me, as I had no clothes except what I had on when we were boarded, my servant very cleverly, as he imagined, having thrown my portmanteau into the man-of-war's boat when he thought I was going to be captured, and all I had in the world was the old serge suit in which I stood. Being without a change and wet through every day and night for six days consecutively, it is little wonder that I caught fever and ague, of which I nearly died in Richmond, and which distressing complaint stuck to me for more than eighteen months. I shall never forget, on going to a store in Wilmington for a new rig-out (which by the by cost $1,200), the look of horror on the storekeeper's face when I told him the coat I had purchased would do if he cut a foot off it; he thought it such a waste of expensive material."

The Three-Funnel Boats

In the latter part of the War between the States, the experience of the blockade runners evolved a superior type of construction for great speed, shallow depth of hold, and increased furnace draught, for which three funnels were provided. A very interesting and unusual sight were these three-funnel boats. I recall their names, *Falcon, Flamingo, Condor, Ptarmigan, Vulture.* Mr. Taylor in his book says that Admiral Hewett commanded the *Falcon* on an ill-fated voyage, but I remember it was the *Condor* and also that one of the passengers was the celebrated and unfortunate lady Mrs. "Greenhow" or "Greenough," who lost her life when the *Condor* ran aground near the bar. The *Condor* went to pieces when she was stranded, the crew escaping to the shore.

Rose O'Neal Greenhow

The *Pevensey*

The last stranded steamer on my list, the *Pevensey*, was probably named for the Earl of Wilmington, who was also Viscount Pevensey.

Her chief officer, who gave his name to his captors as Joseph Brown, was undoubtedly Joseph Brown Long, who ran the blockade many times in the *Cornubia* as chief officer with Captain Burroughs, and as the right-hand man of Maj. Norman S. Walker, the Confederate agent at Bermuda. He was greatly esteemed by all Southerners. I recall his many kindnesses to me with gratefulness.

I quote in full the official reports of the stranding and destruction of the *Pevensey.*

Destruction of the Blockade Runner Pevensey, *June 9, 1864.*
(Report of Acting Volunteer Lieutenant Harris, U. S. Navy.)
"*U.S.S. New Berne,*
"*Hampton Roads, Va., June 16.*

"Sir:

I have the honor to report the stranding, on the 9th instant, of the blockade runner *Pevensey* (named *Penversey* in the extracts April 16, 1864), under the following circumstances:

"3.30 a.m., steering N.E. by N., Beaufort 45 miles distant, made a steamer bearing N.E. by E., 4 miles distant, running slow and heading E.N.E.; she, being to the eastward, did not immediately discover this vessel. Hauled up E.N.E., when, gaining on her within 2 1/2 miles, she made all speed, steering E. Opened fire and stood E by N. The second shot carried away the forward davit of her quarter boat. She immediately changed her course, steered N., and struck the beach 9 miles west of Beaufort at 8.05 a.m. Her crew took to the boats at once, this vessel at the time being 1 1/2 miles distant. Ran into 3 1/2 fathoms, and when within 100 yards of the strand she blew up.

"Sent in three boats, boarded her, and found her engines and boilers completely blown out. Plugged up the pipes; anchored in 3 fathoms, and made arrangements to pull her off; 9 a.m., tug *Violet* came down from Beaufort and anchored on the quarter; 9.30 a.m., Commander B.M. Dove arrived in the *Cherokee*, came on board and said he would take charge of the wreck, and the *New Berne* would proceed to Beaufort, it being then high

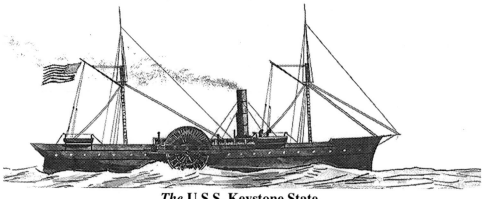

The **U.S.S. Keystone State.**

water, to save the tide in. Recalled boats and arrived at Beaufort at 11 a.m., anchoring outside too late for the tide.

"One prisoner was found on board the vessel, unharmed from the explosion, who proved himself to be an escaped prisoner from Johnson's Island, of Morgan's guerillas. One body was found upon the beach, and thirty-five prisoners were captured on shore by the cavalry, three of whom are supposed to be Confederate officers, one of them adjutant general to Magruder. She was loaded on Confederate account, cargo consisting of arms, blankets, shoes, cloth, clothing, lead, bacon, and numerous packages marked to individuals. She had been chased on the 7th instant by the *Quaker City*, and had thrown overboard, by log book, 30 tons lead and 20 tons bacon; was 543 tons, of English register; no manifest of cargo found. Gunner S.D. Hines has discovered seven Whitworth tompions tied together, bright, and in good condition, which suggests the possibility of that number of guns being under the musket boxes.

"The prisoners captured ashore were held in Fort Macon, and the one secured on board was transferred there by order of Commander Dove. I understood that after the army authorities had satisfied themselves with regard to the identity of the prisoners they were to be transferred to this [place] per *Keystone State.*

"I have learned since leaving Beaufort that the reputed mate is the real captain; that he is a Captain Long, the outdoor agent of Major Walker (the Confederate agent at Bermuda), a citizen of New York, and having formerly commanded a ship from there. The reputed captain (an Englishman) was merely the paper or clearing captain. Of these facts I have informed Captain Gansevoort.

"It will not now be possible to get the vessel off, but a large amount of the cargo can be saved, if properly guarded.

"Had the after 30-pound Parrott, for which the requisition was approved by you April 22, been furnished, his chances of reaching the shore would have been reduced. He evidently was ignorant of his position, as the first question asked was, 'How far is it to Fort Caswell?'

"Very respectfully,
"Your obedient servant,
"T. A. Harris,
"*Acting Volunteer Lieutenant, Commanding.*

"Acting Rear Admiral S. P. Lee,
"*Commanding North Atlantic Blockading Squadron.*"

(Report of Acting Rear Admiral Lee, U.S. Navy.)
"Flagship North Atlantic Blockading Squadron,
"*Washington, D. C., July 14, 1864.*

"Sir:

Inclosed I forward to the Department a list of those of the crew of the blockade runner *Pevensey*, which ran on shore and was destroyed by her crew near Beaufort, N.C., on the 9th ultimo, who are now detained at Camp Hamilton, Fort Monroe, and at Point Lookout. The late master of the *Pevensey* was detained by Captain Gansevoort as a witness, he supposing that a portion of the cargo of the blockade runner was saved and would be sent North as a prize.

"The others are detained as habitual violators of the blockade under the instructions of the Department, dated May 9, 1864, to Rear Admiral Farragut, forwarded to me for my information May 16, 1864.

"The examination of these men took place in presence of Commander Peirce Crosby and Lieut. Commander Chester Hatfield. The chief officer of the *Pevensey*, Joseph Brown, is detained at Camp Hamilton as an habitual violator of the blockade; all the others are detained at Point Lookout. I have requested the commandant of the post at Fort Monroe to discharge the master of the *Pevensey*, as there is no longer any reason for detaining him, the vessel and cargo having proved a total loss.

"I have the honor to be, Sir,

"Very respectfully,
"S. P. Lee,
"Acting Rear Admiral,
"Comdg. North Atlantic Blockading Squadron.

"Hon. Gideon Welles,
Secretary of the Navy."

The *Ella and Annie*

The blockade-runner **Ella and Annie.**

The chief purpose of this book was to record the incidents leading to the stranding of blockade runners upon the Cape Fear coast while endeavoring to elude the Federal cruisers in the War between the States. There were more than three times as many captured or sunk at sea; and a recital of some of these exciting chases would make another volume.

I am tempted, however, to include in these stories of derelicts, an official account of the attempt of the Confederate steamer *Ella and Annie*, in command of Captain Bonneau, with whom I was comparatively intimate, to run down the Federal cruiser *Niphon*, which opposed her entrance into the Cape Fear River, on the 9th of November, 1863, because this incident was of unusual daring on the part of Captain Bonneau, who was liable to be hanged as a pirate for such temerity.

The *Ella and Annie* was subsequently armed and equipped as the U.S. flagship *Malvern* and served that purpose until the end of the war.

(Report of Acting Rear Admiral Lee, U.S. Navy.)

"U.S. Flagship *Minnesota*,
"Off Newport News, Va.,
November 12, 1863.

"Sir:

Captain Frank Bonneau

In addition to the captures of the *Margaret and Jessie* and the *Cornubia*, or *Lady Davis*, detailed in my Nos. 948 and 949 of this date, I have the gratification of presenting to the department the details of the capture of the rebel blockade runner *Ella and Annie*, off Wilmington.

"At 5.30 o'clock on the morning of the 9th instant, the *Niphon*, returning from an unsuccessful chase and steaming along the beach to the northward of New Inlet, made another steamer near Masonboro Inlet coming down along the shore. The stranger finding himself intercepted, put his helm up and endeavored to run down the *Niphon*. This attempt was partly avoided, though the *Niphon* was struck about the fore rigging, and her bowsprit, stem and starboard boats carried away. At the moment of collision Acting Master Breck reports he opened upon the enemy with shell and canister and carried the prize by boarding. A keg of powder and slow match were found ready to blow her up.

"The *Ella and Annie* is represented to be a vessel of 905 tons burden, in good order, with the exception of some small damages from shell and grape.

"Her cargo is chiefly composed of 480 sacks of salt, 500 sacks of saltpeter, 281 cases of Austrian rifles, 500 barrels of beef, 42 cases of paper, etc.

"In the collision three men on board the *Niphon* and four on board the *Ella and Annie* were slightly injured.

"Inclosed is a list of passengers from this prize, brought up by the *New Berne* (thirty-eight in number) and sent to New York in her.

"The capture seems to have been well and gallantly made by Acting Master Breck. Captain Ridgely, senior officer, commends his spirit and promptness. I hope that the department, in view of this especial and other good service on the part of Acting Master Breck, will favorably consider my application for his promotion.

"The *Ella and Annie*, I am informed, was built at Wilmington, Del., is of light draft, fast, and would, I think, be very convenient for general purposes in this squadron, being available either for inside or outside service. I would suggest that she be purchased by Government and sent to this squadron, if, after examination, she be found suitable.

"I have the honor to be, Sir,

"Very respectfully yours,

"S.P. Lee,

"Acting Rear Admiral,

"Comdg. North Atlantic Blockading Squadron.

"Hon. Gideon Welles,

"Secretary of the Navy, Washington, D. C."

(Report of Acting Master Breck, U.S. Navy, Commanding *U.S.S. Niphon.*)

"U.S.S. Niphon,

"Off New Inlet,

"November 9, 1863.

"Sir:

I have the honor to report that on the morning of this date, while near the beach, saw a blockade runner running along the beach; gave chase, fired several guns and rockets, but at last lost sight of her; stood back to my station and steamed along the beach to the north and about 5.30 a.m. saw another steamer running along the shore to the southward; stood in to cut him off, when he turned directly toward me, evidently with the intention of running me down, which I avoided, in part, owing to this vessel answering her helm with great quickness. He struck me forward, both vessels running at great speed. As we came together, I fired a broadside—grape, canister, and shell—and immediately boarded him and took possession. In securing the prisoners a lot of shavings and a slow match attached to a keg of powder were found in the run, the captain acknowledging his intention to destroy the vessel. The collision broke bowsprit, stove all my starboard boats, broke beam, also some planks near the wood ends, damaged guard, chain plates, and caused her decks to leak badly. We have three men wounded; also four of the crew of the Confederate steamer, one dangerously, by grape or shell. The blockade runner, which proved to be the *Ella and Annie*, of Charleston, S.C., is 905 tons; is in good order with the exception of numerous shot holes in her upper works. Her cargo consists, as near as we can ascertain, of rifles, salt, saltpeter, paper, and hardware. She is a Confederate steamer, officered mostly [by men] of the Confederate Navy. She was captured off Masonboro Inlet in four fathoms water, eighteen miles north of Fort Fisher; no vessel in signal distance or in sight immediately after her capture. Steamed toward the fleet, and in about half an hour made the mastheads of a vessel which proved to be the *U.S.S. Shenandoah*, and shortly after seven o'clock came to anchor about three miles north of the senior officer's usual station. About half an hour afterwards the *Shenandoah* came to anchor near us, and contrary to the usual custom the senior officer sent his own prize master on board. Transferred the following officers and crew on board the *Ella and Annie* by order of senior officer: Acting Ensign J. J. Reagean, Acting Third Assistant Engineer J. J. Sullivan, one fireman, one ordinary seaman, three landsmen, and two black refugees.

"Very respectfully,
"Your obedient servant,
"J.B. Breck,
"*Commanding U.S.S. Niphon.*

"Hon. Gideon Welles,
"*Secretary U.S. Navy, Washington, D.C.*"

(Third Report of Acting Master Breck, U.S. Navy, Commanding *U.S.S. Niphon.*)
"*U.S.S. Niphon,*
"*Beaufort, N. C., November 12, 1863.*

"Sir:

In addition to my former report, which was very hurried for want of time, I have to say that F.N. Bonneau, captain of the *Ella and Annie*, states that he has an appointment as lieutenant in the Confederate Navy, and that one of the wounded prisoners, now on shore in the Hospital Beaufort, has an appointment as master in the Confederate Navy, and that all prisoners, except those detained on board of the prize as witnesses, and those in the Hospital Beaufort, were sent by order of Commander Lynch to Fortress Monroe per steamer *New Berne*.

"I wish also to state that no vessels were either in sight or signal distance at the time of the capture of the *Ella and Annie* and that I know nothing more as to her cargo, as the senior officer in command sent an officer who is my senior to command the prize.

"I also find that my damage to this ship is more serious than I at first thought, and will inclose reports from my executive officer and master in regard to the matter.

"The *Niphon* will be hauled up on the sand tomorrow to ascertain the damage done to her, and we are lightening her forward.

"I am, Sir, very respectfully,

"Your obedient servant,
"J.B. Breck,
"Commanding U.S.S. 'Niphon.'

"Acting Rear Admiral S.P. Lee,
"Comdg. North Atlantic Blockading Squadron,
"Off Newport News."

A Near Derelict

This caption with reference to a vessel on fire at sea permits me to describe one of my gallant Captain Maffitt's last runs through the Federal blockade in the War between the States.

It should be borne in mind that the dangers of blockade running materially increased as the enemy became more expert and accumulated facilities to out-wit and out-maneuver the blockade runners. On one of the last voyages of Captain Maffitt he found that the risks were aggravated by the concentration of interest on the part of the Federals to Abaco Light, a night's run from Nassau, and the turning point for blockade runners. Three Federal men-of-war were stationed in the neighborhood and greeted the appearance of the small vessel with a salvo of shot which splintered spars and damaged bulwarks, and would have made short order of the 900 barrels of gunpowder which constituted a portion of the cargo, if the Confederate had not been able, by superior speed facilities, to put a safe distance between her and her pursuers. Hardly out of danger from these three men-of-war, two others were sighted on the horizon, and the race was redoubled as the Federals made a fight for the prize. The same methods used so successfully in the war just concluded in Europe were the best expedients in those days, and Captain Maffitt's ship was saved by following a zig-zag course, which kept the enemy guessing, and finally eluded him altogether. It was after these strenuous experiences of the morning that the lookout announced to the weary officer, "A burning vessel reported aloft."

Surely this was a challenge to the chivalry and humanity of the captain of the hard-pressed Confederate. To the perils of adventure that demanded all his wit and courage were now added the perils of the unknown and the perils of delay and risk to the inflammable cargo. Plainly, however, it was a duty to be faced, not a danger to be evaded, and the captain ordered his ship's course in the direction of the burning vessel. When near enough to discern her character, it was perceived that she was a Spanish barque with ensign at half-mast. From her fore hatch arose a dense smoke, abaft were gathered panic-stricken passengers and crew. The chief mate was dispatched in a cutter to render what assistance might be necessary, and he found on boarding the foreign barque that there were four ladies among the few passengers, and these were calmer than the officers and crew. The latter had completely lost their heads, and in the very act of lowering the long boat were confusedly hauling upon the stay tackle. The Confederate mate went at once to the forecastle, which he instantly deluged with water, to the astonishment of the Spaniards, who had not thought of this method of dealing with the fire which proved so effectual in this case that the flames were soon under control and the fire quickly extinguished.

Three of the ladies were natives of Marblehead, returning from a visit to their uncle in Cuba. They became quite confidential in explaining to the mate their great fears of being captured by Confederate buccaneers with which the waters were infested, according to Cuban rumors. On leaving the boat after rendering this important service, the mate could not refrain from declaring himself one of those awful Confederate slave owners which were the terror of the high seas, but he did not add, as he well might have done, that he was also an officer in command of one of the blockade runners which they so greatly feared. Their amazement was great enough without this bit of information, which might have been passed on by them and given aid and comfort to the enemy.

As the Confederate came into the waters off the coast of North Carolina the dangers were materially increased, because all beacon lights were naturally shrouded to prevent disclosures to the enemy. Ten miles from the bar one of the officers reported to Captain Maffitt his fear that they were in the proximity of the blockaders. The atmosphere was very hazy and to this they owed the possibility of escape, for two cruisers were at anchor just ahead of them and there was no course to pursue except the perilous one of running between the enemy ships. The Federals were immediately aware of this daring maneuver, and a fiery rocket revealed the Confederate and the moment's flare of a calcium light was followed by the curt demand of a Federal officer, "Heave to, or I'll sink you."

In this case discretion was the better part of valor, and Captain Maffitt gave the order in a voice loud enough to be heard by foe as well as friend. Assured that the Confederate captain was complying with orders, the enemy did not suspect that the order that had been so plainly heard was merely a ruse and that the engineer had received whispered instructions, "Full speed ahead, sir, and open your throttle valve." The movements of the paddle deceived the Federals into the belief that the Confederate was really backing, but just as the advantage was with the blockade runner and her clever scheme was detected, fire was opened upon her with relentless fury. Drummond lights were burned, doubtless to aid the artilleryists, but so radiated the mist as to raise the hull above the line of vision, and the destructive missiles were poured into the sparse rigging and the hull was spared injury. Thus the blockade runner escaped from the foe and delivered 900 barrels of gunpowder to the Confederates at Wilmington, and this ammunition was used afterwards by General Johnston at the battle of Shiloh.

A Human Derelict

The story of disasters on Cape Fear during the Federal blockade, 1861-1865, would be incomplete without reference to a human tragedy, the drowning of an accomplished Southern woman, Mrs. Rose O'Neal Greenhow. Mrs. Greenhow was a prominent figure in Washington society during the Buchanan administration. She had become a resident of Washington in her girlhood, and had grown to womanhood under the influences which are thrown around the society element in the Nation's

Capital. She was rich, beautiful, and attractive, possessing a ready wit and a charming and forceful personality. She was a close personal friend of President Buchanan and a friend of William H. Seward. With such friends her social position was of the highest, and she entertained many of the most prominent men in the country in her hospitable home.

When the War between the States began she was entertaining Col. Thomas Jordan, later Adjutant General of the Confederate Army. Knowing well Mrs. Greenhow's strong sympathy for the land of her birth, Colonel Jordan determined to secure her services for the newborn Confederacy, and proposed to her that she become a secret agent for his government. Her social position, her wide acquaintance, her personal magnetism made her preeminently the one to extract information of military value for the Southern cause. Mrs. Greenhow consented to perform this perilous service for the land she loved, and started at once to get possession of facts which would be useful in the coming campaign.

Col. Thomas Jordan, CSA

She began her work in April, 1861, and by November Allan Pinkerton, head of the Federal Secret Service, sent in a report to the War Department vehemently inveighing against Mrs. Rose Greenhow for alienating the hearts of Federal officers from their sympathy with their country, and accusing her of obtaining through her wiles and powerful personal methods memoranda (and maps) which could only have been known to officials of the Federal Government.

When the cry "On to Richmond!" was raised, it was absolutely essential for the Confederate Army under General Beauregard to have definite information about the point of attack. This data was furnished him by Mrs. Greenhow. She advised him that the enemy would advance across the Potomac and on Manassas, via Fairfax Court House and Centerville.

The Federal Army delayed the advance, and a second messenger was sent to Mrs. Greenhow, who was able to add to her previous information, and on the strength of it Johnston was ordered to reînforce Beauregard with the last of his 8,500 men, and the wavering Federal Army turned back and fled in a rout—a mob of panic-stricken fugitives. It was soon known in Washington that Mrs. Greenhow had supplied the information upon which the Confederates had constructed their plans, and she was closely watched. Long after she knew that she must some day be arrested, she continued her activities, finding opportunities every day to communicate with Confederate officers, and her services were so valuable that she could not be persuaded to take refuge in the Confederate lines when there was so much work for her to do in the Federal Capital.

The Old Capitol Prison

She was in her own home when she was finally placed under arrest. Here she was closely guarded, but a friend and her little daughter were permitted to remain with her. In spite of the heavy guard, she continued to comunicate with Southern messengers and kept them informed of what she heard. After a few months she was transferred to the Old Capitol Prison and kept in confinement with her child in a room 10 by 12. She suffered keenly in this cold and cheerless place. The soldiers who guarded her were very strict, but in spite of their closest scrutiny she managed under their very eyes to send messages to the people who were eagerly awaiting news of her on the other side of the lines. After tedious months of imprisonment she was tried* on the charge of treason. There was much direct and indirect evidence against her, but her attitude was uncompromising, and after the trial she was permitted to make her way through the lines to Richmond, where she spent some time until she took passage in a blockade runner with her daughter, whom she wished to place in a convent in Paris. She took with her letters to Mason and Slidell, which

*There are no formal records available to verify this.

requested that every courtesy be shown her. In Paris she was given a private audience with Napoleon III.

While Mrs. Greenhow was in England her book, *My Imprisonment, or The First Year of Abolition Rule in Washington*, was published and created a sensation. It was a vehicle for the most pronounced propaganda for the cause of the Confederacy and served it well. Not a little sympathy was created for the South by this book of personal experience.

While in London Mrs. Greenhow became engaged to a nobleman and she expected to return and marry him after a voyage to America. In August, 1864, she took passage on the *Condor* and there is strong reason to suppose that her business in Wilmington was in the interests of the Confederacy.

Rose Greenhow's boat leaving the **Condor.**

The *Condor* arrived opposite the mouth of the river on the night of September 30, but as she crept up the river, the pilot saw an object about 200 yards from shore which he thought was an enemy vessel, and he swerved his course and ran his vessel on New Inlet Bar. The object was the *Night Hawk*, a blockade runner which had been run down the previous night, and the *Condor* might have completed the trip in safety. Mrs. Greenhow and her party begged the captain to send them ashore in a boat, as this seemed the only chance of escape from a second arrest as a spy. The captain acceded to her request, and the boat put off. It capsized, however, and Mrs. Greenhow, weighted by her clothing and a quantity of golden sovereigns, was drowned a few yards from land.

Greenhow's tombstone in Wilmington, N.C.'s Oakdale Cemetery.

Her body washed ashore the next day and was found by Mr. Thomas E. Taylor, who afterwards took it to Wilmington. She was laid out in the Seamen's Bethel, beautiful in death as she had been in life. She was wrapped in the Confederate flag and with full honors of war interred in Oakdale Cemetery, where a small cross bearing her name may be seen to this day.

After the funeral her personal effects and the articles she had brought with her from abroad were sold at public auction. It was said that an English countess or duchess had an interest in the speculation and was to have shared the profits.

Tales of the Sea

A Confederate Daughter

The following extract from *Southern Historical Papers*, written about the year 1890, by Colonel Lamb, the commander of Fort Fisher, gives a glimpse of the social side of life at the fort during the War between the States and of some of the distinguished gentlemen who were drawn into this dangerous traffic by a love of adventure, by sentiment, or by sympathy with the Confederate cause, and by the promise of large profits for successful enterprises.

"In the fall of 1857 a lovely Puritan maiden, still in her teens, was married in Grace Church, Providence, R. I., to a Virginia youth, just passed his majority, who brought her to his home in Norfolk, a typical ancestral homestead, where, beside the 'white folks,' there was quite a colony of family servants, from the pickaninny just able to crawl to the old gray-headed mammy who had nursed 'ole massa.' She soon became enamoured of her surroundings and charmed with the devotion of her colored maid, whose sole duty it was to wait upon her young missis. When the John Brown

Sarah Chaffee "Daisy" Lamb and child.

raid burst upon the South and her husband was ordered to Harpers Ferry, there was not a more indignant matron in all Virginia, and when at last secession came, the South did not contain a more enthusiastic little rebel.

"On the 15th of May, 1862, a few days after the surrender of Norfolk to the Federals by her father-in-law, then mayor, amid the excitement attending a captured city, her son Willie was born. Cut off from her husband and subjected to the privations and annoyances incident to a subjugated community, her father insisted upon her coming with her children to his home in Providence; but, notwithstanding she was in a luxurious home with all that paternal love could do for her, she preferred to leave all these comforts to share with her husband the dangers and privations of the South. She vainly tried to persuade Stanton, Secretary of War, to let her and her three children with a nurse return to the South; finally he consented to let her go by flag of truce from Washington to City Point, but without a nurse, and as she was unable to manage three little ones, she left the youngest with his grandparents, and with two others bravely set out for Dixie. The generous outfit of every description which was prepared for the journey, and which was carried to the place of embarkation, was ruthlessly cast aside by the inspectors on the wharf, and no tears or entreaties or offers of reward by the parents availed to pass anything save a scanty supply of clothing and other necessaries.

Arriving in the South, the brave young mother refused the proffer of a beautiful home in Wilmington, the occupancy of the grand old colonial mansion Orton, on the Cape Fear River, and insisted upon taking up her abode with her children and their colored nurse in the upper room of a pilot's house, where they lived until the soldiers of the garrison built her a cottage one mile north of Fort Fisher, on the Atlantic Beach. In both of these homes she was occasionally exposed to the shot and shell fired from blockaders at belated blockade runners.

"It was a quaint abode, constructed in most primitive style, with three rooms around one big chimney, in which North Carolina pine knots supplied heat and light on winter nights. This cottage became historic, and was famed for the frugal but tempting meals which its charming hostess would prepare for her distinguished guests. Besides the

The Lamb cottage near Fort Fisher.

many illustrious Confederate Army and Navy officers who were delighted to find this bit of sunshiny civilization on the wild sandy beach, ensconced among the sand dunes and straggling pines and black-jack, many celebrated English naval officers enjoyed its hospitality under assumed names: Roberts,

Charles Hobart-Hampden

afterwards the renowned Hobart Pasha, who commanded the Turkish Navy; Murray, now Admiral Murray-Aynsley, long since retired after having been rapidly promoted for gallantry and meritorious services in the British Navy; the brave but unfortunate Hugh Burgoyne, V. C., who went down in the British iron-clad *Captain*, in the Bay of Biscay; and the chivalrous Hewett, who won the Victoria Cross in the Crimea and was knighted for his services as ambassador to King John of Abyssinia, and who, after commanding the Queen's yacht, died lamented as Admiral

Hewett. Besides these there were many genial and gallant merchant captains, among them Halpin, who afterwards commanded the *Great Eastern* while laying ocean cables; and famous war correspondents—Hon. Francis C. Lawley, M. P., correspondent of the *London Times*, and Frank Vizetelly, of the *London Illustrated News*, afterwards murdered in the Soudan. Nor must the plucky Tom Taylor be forgotten, supercargo of the *Banshee* and the *Night Hawk*, who, by his coolness and daring escaped with a boat's crew from the hands of the Federals after capture off the fort, and who was endeared to the children as the Santa Claus of the war.

"At first the little Confederate was satisfied with pork and potatoes, cornbread and rye coffee, with sorghum sweetening; but after the blockade runners made her acquaintance the impoverished storeroom was soon filled to overflowing, notwithstanding her heavy requisitions on it for the post hospital, the sick and wounded soldiers and sailors always being a subject of her tenderest solicitude, and often the hard-worked and poorly fed colored hands blessed the little lady of the cottage for a tempting treat.

Rear Amiral David Dixon Porter.

"Full of stirring events were the two years passed in the cottage on Confederate Point. The drowning of Mrs. Rose Greenhow, the famous Confederate spy, off Fort Fisher, and the finding of her body, which was tenderly cared for, and the rescue from the waves, half dead, of Professor Holcombe, and his restoration, were incidents never to be forgotten. Her fox hunting with horse and hounds, the narrow escapes of friendly vessels, the fights over blockade runners driven ashore, the execution of deserters, and the loss of an infant son, whose little spirit went out with the tide one sad summer night, all contributed to the reality of this romantic life.

"When Porter's fleet appeared off Fort Fisher, December, 1864, it was storm bound for several days, and the little family with their household goods were sent across the river to Orton before Butler's powder ship blew up. After the Christmas victory over Porter and Butler, the little heroine insisted upon coming back to her cottage, although her husband had procured a home of refuge in Cumberland County. General Whiting protested against her running the risk, for on dark nights her husband could not leave the fort, but she said if the firing became too hot she would run behind the sand hills as she had done before, and come she would.

"The fleet reappeared unexpectedly on the night of the 12th of January, 1865. It was a dark night, and when the lights of the fleet were reported her husband sent a courier to the cottage to instruct her to pack up quickly and be prepared to leave with children and nurse as soon as he could come to bid them good-bye. The garrison barge, with a trusted crew, was stationed at Craig's Landing, near the cottage. After midnight, when all necessary orders were given for the coming attack, the colonel mounted his horse and rode to the cottage, but all was dark and silent. He found the message had been delivered, but his brave wife had been so undisturbed by the news that she had fallen asleep and no preparations for a retreat had been made. Precious hours had been lost, and as the fleet would soon be shelling the beach and her husband have to return to the fort, he hurried them into the boat as soon as dressed, with only what could be gathered up hastily, leaving dresses, toys, and household articles to fall into the hands of the foe."

Mr. Thomas E. Taylor's description of the famous Englishmen referred to is worth repeating:

Captain Hugh Burgoyne.

"As my memory takes me back to those jovial but hard-working days of camaraderie, it is melancholy to think how many of those friends have gone before; Mrs. Murray-Aynsley, Mrs. Hobart and her husband, Hobart Pasha; Hugh Burgoyne, one of the Navy's brightest ornaments, who was drowned while commanding the ill-fated *Captain;* Hewett, who lately gave up command of the Channel Fleet only to die; old Steele, the king of blockade-running captains; Maurice Portman, an ex-diplomatist; Frank Vizetelly, whose bones lie alongside those of Hicks Pasha in the Soudan; Lewis Grant Watson, my brother agent; Arthur Doering, one of my loyal lieutenants, and a host of old Confederate friends, are all gone, and I could count on my fingers those remaining of a circle of chums who did not know what care or fear was, and who would have stood by each other through thick and thin in any emergency. In fact, my old friends Admiral Murray-Aynsley and Frank Hurst are almost the only two living of that companionship.

"Of Hobart Pasha and of the important part he played in the Turko-Russian war and Cretan rebellion (in which he acknowledged that his blockade-running experiences stood him in such good stead) most, if not all

British war artist Frank Vizetelly.

my readers will have read or heard. He commanded a smart little twin-screw steamer called the *Don*, in fact one of the first twin-propeller steamers ever built. And very proud he was of his craft, in which he made several successful runs under the assumed name of Captain Roberts. On her first trip after Captain Roberts gave up command in order to go home, the *Don* was captured after a long chase, and his late chief officer, who was then in charge, was assumed by his captors to be Roberts. He maintained silence concerning the point, and the Northern newspapers upon the arrival of the prize at Philadelphia were full of the subject of the 'Capture of the *Don* and the notorious English naval officer, "Captain Roberts." ' Much chagrined were they to find they had got the wrong man, and that the English naval officer was still at large.

"Poor Burgoyne, whose tragic and early end, owing to the capsizing of the *Captain*, everybody deplored, as a blockade runner was not very successful. If I remember correctly he made only two or three trips. Had he lived he would have had a brilliant career before him in the Navy; bravest of the brave, as is evidenced by the V. C. he wore, gentle as a woman, unselfish to a fault, he might have saved his life if he had thought more of himself and less of his men on that terrible occasion off Finisterre, when his last words were, 'Look out for yourselves, men; never mind me.'

"Then there was Hewett, another wearer of the 'cross for valor,' who has only recently joined the majority, after a brilliant career as admiral commanding in the East Indies, Red Sea, and Channel Fleet; who successfully interviewed King John in Abyssinia, and was not content to pace the deck of his flagship at Suakim, but insisted upon fighting in the square at El Teb, and whose hospitality and geniality later on as commander in chief of the Channel Fleet was proverbial.

"Murray-Aynsley, I rejoice to say, is still alive.* Who that knows 'old Murray' does not love him? Gentle as a child, brave as a lion, a man without guile, he was perhaps the most successful of all the naval blockade runners. In the *Venus* he had many hairbreadth escapes, notably on one occasion when he ran the gauntlet of the Northern fleet in daylight into Wilmington. The *Venus*, hotly pursued by several blockaders and pounded at by others, while she steamed straight through them, old Murray on the bridge, with his coat sleeves hitched up almost to his arm-pits—a trick he had when greatly excited—otherwise as cool as possible, was, as Lamb afterwards told me, 'a sight never to be forgotten.' "

---

* They are all gone now.—J. S.

Intelligent Contrabands

An almost daily incident of the Federal blockading fleet was the rescue from frail boats of negro slaves, officially reported by the Federals as "intelligent contrabands," who at the risk of their lives deserted their owners and escaped to the Federal warships several miles from the beach. They numbered several hundred during the war, and I am informed that very few of them returned from the North, where many settled in their new-found freedom. Some of the more industrious prospered, but a larger proportion died from exposure to the rigorously cold winters of the North.

Specimens of the official reports of such cases follow:

"*U.S.S. Monticello,*
"Off Wilmington, N. C.,
"*September 22, 1862.*

"Sir:
I beg leave to forward you the following information obtained from the within named persons, who came off to this vessel this morning:

"Frank Clinton, aged thirty-five years, belonging to Robert H. Cowan.
"Samuel Mince, aged twenty-three years, belonging to Mrs. Elizabeth Mints.
"Thomas Cowen, aged twenty-four years, belonging to Mrs. J. G. Wright.
"Charles Millett, aged twenty-eight years, belonging to Mrs. John Walker.
"James Brown, aged twenty-three years, belonging to John Brown.
"Horace Smith, aged twenty-two years, belonging to Mrs. William Smith.
"David Mallett, aged twenty-six years, belonging to Mrs. John Walker.

"The gunboat *North Carolina* is to be launched next Saturday and is to be clad with railroad iron down to the water's edge. The sides of the boat are built angular, and the guns are to be mounted on a covered deck. The lower part of the hull is of pine and the upper of heavy oak. This vessel is to be fitted up by Mr. Benjamin Beery and the engine she is to have is to come out of the steamer *Uncle Ben*, formerly a tugboat. The contrabands state that they are sanguine of having her ready by the 10th of October, 1862. These contrabands are from in and about Wilmington city, and they all agree in stating that that city is completely entrenched and guns mounted at every half mile upon the works. From their account Cape Fear River has several batteries upon its banks. The first is called Camp Brown, two miles from the city, which is an earth and log work on the right-hand side going up the river, and mounts two guns; opposite to it are obstructions in the river, consisting of sunken cribs. The next fort below is called Mount Tirza and mounts two guns and is on the same side of the river. The next is Fort St. Philip, a large work, mounting sixteen guns, near Old Brunswick, on the left-hand side of the river going up. Opposite this last-named work the

The **C.S.S. North Carolina,** *as drawn by Dan Dowdy.*

obstructions in the river are heavy piles with a narrow passageway through them. At this point the lightboat, which was taken from Frying Pan Shoals, is anchored inside the obstruction and mounts four guns. There is also a lightboat anchored inside Zeek's Island, mounting a like number of guns. One of these contrabands is from Fayetteville, N.C., and states that they are making rifles and gun carriages up there, and also that they are building a large foundry and blacksmith's shop. As fast as the arms are completed they are sent to Raleigh, North Carolina.

"These contrabands state that the rebels succeeded in getting out of the *Modern Greece* (which vessel was run ashore near New Inlet) six rifled cannon, which, from their description, I should judge to be Withworth's breech-loading guns; also 500 stand of arms and a large amount of powder and clothing, the last two in a damaged condition. One also states that the steamer *Kate*, before running into this port, was chased by a cruiser and threw overboard 10,000 stand of arms. This he is positive of, as one of the hands on board the *Kate*, a friend of his, told him so. From their accounts I judge that a regular and uninterrupted trade is kept up between Nassau, New Providence, and Shallotte

LtCmdr. D. L. Braine, U.S. Navy

Inlet, N.C., which inlet is about 20 miles to the westward of this place. Schooners are said to arrive here weekly, and, after discharging, take in cotton, turpentine, and rosin, and sail for Nassau with papers purporting that they sailed from the city of Wilmington. I would suggest that some means be taken to stop this trade, and I am,

"Very respectfully,
"Your obedient servant,
"D. L. Braine,
"Lieutenant-Commander.

"U.S. Gunboat *Penobscot,*
"Off Cape Fear, N.C.,
"September 23, 1862.

"Sir:
   I have to inform you that seven contrabands came to this vessel this morning who gave their own and their masters' names as follows:

"William, owned by S.G. Northrop, of Wilmington.
"Lewis, owned by Dr. McCrea, of Wilmington.
"Ben Greer, owned by P.K. Dickinson, of Wilmington.
"George, owned by T.D. Walker, of Wilmington.
"Virgil Richardson, owned by James Bradley.
"Abraham Richardson, owned by D.A.F. Flemming.

 "No information of importance was elicited, except that the steamer *Mariner*, loaded with cotton, tobacco, and turpentine, was ready for sea and would make an early attempt to run the blockade of this port.
                              "I am, respectfully,
                              "Your obedient servant,
                                   "J. M. B. Clitz,
                                        Commander.

"Commander G.H. Scott,
"Commanding U.S.S. Maratanza,
"And Senior Officer Present."

   "From William Robins, contraband, ship carpenter, who has been at work upon one of the rebel gunboats at Wilmington since July:

"**1.** There are two boats in process of construction; one at J.L. Cassidy & Sons, the other at Beery & Brothers. Captain Whitehead superintends the former and Mr. Williams the latter. Commander Muse has control of the whole. Both boats are built upon the same plan, 150 feet keel, 23 feet beam, 12 feet draft. They are to be iron-roofed like the *Merrimac.* The iron is to be made in Richmond and will be ready in four months. The engines are on board but not set. One of them is new, made at Richmond; the other was

The ironclad C.S.S. Merrimac.

taken from the *Uncle Ben*. Propellers are about eight feet in diameter. The boats are pierced for eight guns, but will carry but three, which can be moved at ease. Guns are not yet ready. Boats would have been ready for launching in three weeks had not many of the workmen left. Some struck for more pay; some were fearful of yellow fever. Formerly ninety-five to one hundred were at work on each boat; now only thirty. Pay $2.50 to $3.

"**2.** Provisions scarce. Flour, $27; rice, 12 1/2 cents; potatoes, $3.50 to $4; bacon, 50 cents; beef, 25 cents; meal, $2; butter, 85 cents to $1.

"**3.** There are no soldiers in Wilmington. Colonel Livingsthrop (Leventhorpe), with one regiment, is at Masonboro Sound. There are about 3,000 in all in this vicinity. Colonel Lamb is at Fort Fisher. Captain Dudley evacuated Zeek's Island and is now at Fort Fisher.

"**4.** Friday last was set apart by President Davis as a day for thanksgiving and prayer for the victories before Richmond and in Maryland, as also for the capture of Harpers Ferry and Cincinnati, both of which were taken without the loss of a life.

"5. No vessel has run in or out of the port since the *Modern Greece* except the *Kate*. The *Modern Greece* had two shots through her boiler, and one through her donkey engine. Her cargo consisted of powder and arms and whisky. Much was taken out and much remains. Powder was all wet. They dried some of it. She had two heavy guns. She was a very fine steamer. They saved none of her machinery.

"The *Kate* ran in and out the main channel. The tug *Mariner* is now ready to run out, having 100 bales of cotton and 100 barrels of rosin. They say a schooner ran in at Little River Inlet not long ago. The *Mariner* is going to Nassau for salt."

Information given by Colonel Shaw's body servant:

"Thirty-five hundred troops (a large margin given) in and about Wilmington, including all the forts, under the command of General Leventhorpe. At present most of the soldiers have left Wilmington and moved down this way on account of yellow fever. There are about 800 at Fort Caswell, and about double the number at Fort Fisher. The troops are clothed, very dirty, but apparently are sufficiently fed. Provisions come to them from the country. They enlist from fourteen to fifty years of age. Many of the conscripts run away; 300 have deserted in one day. Have telegrams from Richmond, but they are in doubt about the entire correctness of such. Previous to the battles before Richmond the people were quite disheartened and were willing to give up the place; since, however, they are much encouraged, and a better feeling pervades. There are some Union men in W. Not any small craft at W. The two gunboats, not rams, are being completed; workmen from the army. One engine is new from Richmond; the other old from *Uncle Ben*, and each boat will mount three guns on a side; also one forward and one aft. The tug *Mariner* is prepared to run for Nassau. Has two guns; is loaded with cotton. Flour is $30 per barrel; whisky $15 a gallon; boots $20 a pair. Have grown some corn about W. this season. No business doing. Clerks all enlisted. The fort's southwest breastworks were injured by the *Otorara;* no one killed. Beauregard at Charleston, and Lieut. Commander Flusser, who ought to have left out the 'l' in his name, said: 'A "reliable contraband" who says he deserted from the enemy today and who represents himself as an officer's servant, declares that he has heard of no boat building up this river; that he does not believe that there is one there; that one was some time since under construction at Tarboro, but that work on her has been discontinued,' etc. I fear the 'reliable contraband' was sent in by *Messieurs les Secesh.* I do not think anyone can outlie a North Carolina white, unless he be a North Carolina negro."

Also there were occasional white deserters from Fort Fisher and from the out-lying Confederate camps or outposts. These were not named for obvious reasons, and they were described in the official reports as so ragged and so infested with vermin that they had to be immediately divested of their clothing, which was thrown overboard, and the deserters were clothed from the ships' supply chests. As cleanliness is said to be next to godliness, it is manifest that these fellows were a very bad lot.

Malingerers

It is remarkable that the blockade runners seldom included in their complement of officers and crew a professional doctor or surgeon, although there were occasions when they were greatly needed. Few of our men were wounded, although the bombshells burst all round us again and again and finally sunk the *Lilian* to a level with the deck.

The runs from Wilmington to Nassau were made in forty-eight to fifty-two hours, and to Bermuda in seventy-two to eighty hours, and the sick or wounded received scant attention until they reached port. It therefore devolved upon the purser or the chief officer to attend such cases, and my very limited knowledge of medicine restricted the treatment of our alleged sick men to compound cathartic pills and quinine. A majority of the cases of "pains all over them" were malingerers, some of whom dodged their duty during the entire voyage. Captain Hobart, of the *Don*, told us of such a case on his ship interviewed by his chief officer, C—, as follows:

C.: "Well, my man, what's the matter with you?"
Patient: "Please, sir, I've got pains all over me."
C.: "Oh, all over you, are they? That's bad."

Then during the pause it was evident that something was being mixed up, and I could hear C— say: "Here, take this, and come again in the evening." (Exit patient.)

Then C— said to himself: "I don't think he'll come again; he has got two drops of the croton. Skulking rascal, pains all over him, eh?"

"I never heard the voice of that patient again," said Captain Hobart; "in fact, after a short time we had no cases of sickness on board."

C— explained that what he served out, as he called it, was croton oil; and that none of the crew came twice for treatment.

The ship's discipline was generally well maintained at sea, but instances of insubordination in port were of almost daily occurrence. These were dealt with usually by the first mate, or, as he was designated, the chief officer. But some of the incorrigibles were brought before the commander for treatment and something like this colloquy, which I take partly from *Punch*, would ensue:

Commander: "What is this man's character apart from this offence?"

Petty Officer: "Well, sir, this here man, he goes ashore when he likes, he comes aboard when he likes, he uses 'orrible language when he's spoke to. In fact from his general behavior he might be taken for the captain of this ship," which exactly fitted the case of our skipper at that time, who was an expert in the use of 'orrible language.

Experiences In Quarantine

E luding the blockading fleet at the Cape Fear Bar was not the only adventure in those perilous days. It was quite within the range of possibility that a steamer would run into a harbor and find the town, hitherto perfectly healthy, withered under the malign spell of some scourge like yellow fever or smallpox. Sometimes the plague would break out in the town while the steamer was loading, sometimes it would break out among the crew of the steamer, and this is what was alleged of the *Lilian* on the occasion I am about to relate.

After several narrow escapes from the squadron in the Gulf Stream, the *Lilian* made St. George, Bermuda, on the morning of the fourth day, and at once discharged her cargo, hoping to get away in time for another run while we had a few hours of darkness.

We had, however, hardly received the half of our inward cargo of gunpowder and commissary supplies when we were visited by the harbor doctor, who alleged that we had a case of smallpox on board and peremptorily ordered us to the quarantine ground, about two miles out of port, among some uninhabited rocks, which made the usual dreariness of a quarantine station more distressing, and where he informed us we must remain at least twenty-one days. In vain our captain protested that he was mistaken, that the case to which he referred was a slight attack of malarial fever, combined with other symptoms which were not at all dangerous (which subsequently proved to be true). The doctor was unrelenting; if we did not proceed at once, he said, he would report us to the governor at Hamilton, who would send *H.M.S. Spitfire*, then on the station, to tow us out, and after we had served our quarantine, we would be arrested for resisting his authority. Finding remonstrance of no avail, our captain agreed to get away as soon as possible, but before we could make preparation for our departure a tug was sent alongside which towed us out, *nolens volens*, and left us at anchor among the sea gulls, with only ten days' provisions for a three weeks' quarantine.

Being ex officio the ship's doctor, I began at once to physic the unfortunate sailor who had unwittingly brought us into this trouble, and, although my knowledge of the pharmacopúia did not go beyond cathartic pills and quinine, I soon had him on his feet to join all hands for inspection by the quarantine officer, who came off to windward of us every day and at a respectable distance bawled out his category of questions which were required by law.

We were daily warned that if any of our officers or crew were found on shore or on board any of the vessels in the harbor, the full extent of the law would be meted out to them, and we were given to understand that twenty-one days' quarantine was a mere bagatelle compared with the punishment which would follow any attempt to evade these restrictions; notwithstanding which, we came to a unanimous decision at the end of three days that we would prefer the risk of capture at sea to such a life in comparative security, and it was accordingly resolved by the captain that if any of us were plucky enough to take his gig and a boat's crew to St. George and secure some castings at a shipsmith's on shore which were required by the chief engineer, we would proceed toward Wilmington without further preparation and without the formality required by law.

Being comparatively indifferent as to the result, albeit somewhat confident of success, I at once volunteered, to which our captain agreed, and amid a good deal of chaffing from several Confederate officers who were with us as passengers, I started with our second engineer and five trustworthy men for the shore.

We were careful to leave shortly after the visit of the health physician, so that our absence would not be noticed when all hands were turned out, and as we approached the harbor I was gratified to observe that we were entirely unnoticed. We landed about half a mile below the town, and leaving the men with the boat, which I ordered them to keep concealed, I proceeded with the engineer to dispatch our business, which delayed us several hours.

At last we were ready for the return, and finding our men unmolested, we proceeded down the harbor toward the ship *Storm King*, which had recently left the China trade to carry Confederate States Government cotton from the Bermuda rendezvous to Liverpool. As we passed under her quarter, we were excitedly hailed by her captain, to whom I was well known personally, with the intelligence that a quarantine boat had just left our ship and that we were probably discovered, as its course had been suddenly changed for us while we were pulling down the bay.

Thinking to elude the pursuer, if such it proved to be, I steered for the rocks along shore, the men giving way at the oars with a will, but we soon saw that we were closely watched and that our friend's fears were fully realized. The well-known yellow flag was borne by a boat now clearly in pursuit of us; and, finding escape cut off, we at once returned to the *Storm King* and entreated the captain to secrete us on board, and if the health officer boarded him, to profess ignorance of us altogether. This the good fellow agreed to do, and my men having been set to work as if they were part of the crew, I, with the engineer, was at once secreted and locked in one of the many staterooms then empty.

We had hardly settled ourselves in the berths, determined that if the worst came we would cover up our heads and draw the curtains, when we heard the measured sound of oars approaching the gangway near the room in which we were hiding, and a moment later the hail, "*Storm King* ahoy!"

"Aye, aye, sir; what do you want?"

"You have on board a boat's crew from the steamer *Lilian* in quarantine, who have left contrary to law. I demand their surrender."

"Quite a mistake, Doctor; quite a mistake, I assure you," responded Captain McDonald.

"But I saw the boat pull under your quarter a few minutes ago, and I insist upon their forthcoming, or we will search your ship."

"But I protest, Doctor, there are no such people on board my ship."

"What a consummate liar old McDonald is," groaned the engineer, sweltering under two pairs of blankets.

"Ah ha," exclaimed the health officer at this moment, "we have here the captain's gig alongside; and here is the name *Lilian* on the stern. How is this?"

"Oh," replied the imperturbable McDonald, "we picked her up adrift this morning; I am glad to know the owner."

"A very unlikely story, Captain, and we will have to search," quoth the doctor; and then we heard several persons ascending the ladder, followed by further expostulations on the part of our friend the captain, evidently of no avail, for the party immediately entered the saloon and began their search. Door after door was opened and shut, and as they gradually approached our hiding place, I looked up at Sandy McKinnon, the Scotch engineer, who presented a most ludicrous and woeful sight, the perspiration pouring down his fat cheeks, as in a most despairful voice he moaned, "It's a' up wi' us the noo, Purser, it's a' up wi' us; we shall be put in preeson and the deil kens what'll be to pay."

With anxious hearts we waited for the worst, and at last it came; a heavy hand wrenched our door knob and an impatient voice demanded that the door be unlocked. The steward protested that the room was empty and that the key was lost, which only seemed to increase the officer's determination to enter. High words ensued. The captain, with a heartiness which excited our admiration but increased our fear, poured a volley of abuse upon the unlucky doctor, who was apparently discharging his duty, and at times I fancied they had almost come to blows. This was at last quelled by a peremptory demand that the ship's carpenter be sent for to force the door. The steward at this juncture produced the key, which he averred had just been found in another lock, and while he fumbled at our door I thought I heard the sound of suppressed laughter on the outside, but dismissed the idea as absurd.

A moment after the door opened, and before our astonished vision were ranged our good friends and shipmates, Major Hone of Savannah, Capt. Leo Vogel of St. Augustine, Sergeant Gregory of Crowels, and Eugene Maffitt, who with Captain McDonald and several of his friends were fairly shrieking with laughter at our sorry plight. We had been completely sold. The whole scheme was planned on board our own ship immediately after our departure, and Captain McDonald was privy to the arrangement which he so successfully carried out.

The voices which we supposed in our fright came from Her Majesty's officers, were feigned by our own people, who made the most of the joke at our expense. The trick was too good to keep, and when the good doctor came next day to discharge us from quarantine, all traces of sickness having disappeared, no one enjoyed the fun more than he, although he said it might have resulted seriously enough.

Confederate States Signal Corps

The Confederate States Signal Corps frequently rendered some very efficient service to the blockade runners after they had succeeded in getting between the blockaders and the beach, where they were also in danger of the shore batteries until their character became known to the forts.

As the signal system developed, a detailed member was sent out with each ship, and so important did this service become that signal officers, as they were called, were occasionally applied for by owners or captains of steamers in the Clyde or at Liverpool before sailing for Bermuda or Nassau to engage in running the blockade.

The first attempt to communicate with the shore batteries was a failure, and consequently the service suffered some reproach for a while, but subsequent practice with intelligent, cool-headed men resulted in complete success, and some valuable ships, with still more valuable cargoes, were saved from capture or destruction by the intervention of the signal service,

Price's Creek Lighthouse in 2006.

when, owing to the darkness and bad landfall, the captain and pilot were alike unable to recognize their geographical position.

To the late Mr. Frederick W. Gregory, of Crowells, N.C., belonged the honor of the first success as a signal operator in this service. Identified with the corps from the beginning of the blockade, and with the Cape Fear at Price's Creek Station, which was for a long time in his efficient charge, he brought to this new and novel duty an experience and efficiency equalled by few of his colleagues and surpassed by none. It was well said of him that he was always ready and never afraid, two elements of the almost unvarying success which attended the ships to which he was subsequently assigned. It was my good fortune to be intimately associated with Mr. Gregory for nearly two years, during which we had many ups and downs together as shipmates aboard and as companions ashore. He was one of the few young men engaged in blockade running who successfully resisted the evil influences and depraved associations with which we were continually surrounded. Unselfish and honorable in all his relations with his fellows, courageous as a lion in time of danger, he was an honor to his State and to the cause which he so worthily represented.

The following narrative related by him gives a more explicit account of the signal service than I could offer by description of its workings:

"Some time early in 1863, the Confederate Government purchased on the Clyde (I think) two steamers for the purpose of running the blockade. The first to arrive was the *Giraffe*. While in the Cape Fear, Captain Alexander, who had charge of the signal corps at Smithville, suggested the propriety of putting a signal officer aboard to facilitate the entrance of ships into the port

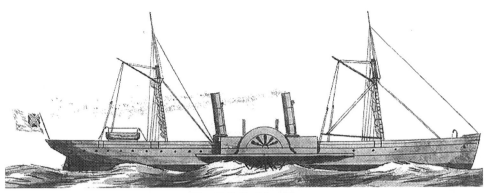

The **C.S.S. Giraffe.**

at night by the use of two lights, a red and a white, covered with a shade in front of the globe to lift up and down, by which we could send messages as we did with the flag on land in the day and with the torch at night; the red light representing the wave to the right and the white light the wave to the left. After some consultation General Whiting ordered Captain Alexander to send up a signal officer to join the *Giraffe*, and Robert Herring was detailed for that purpose and sent to Wilmington, where the lights were prepared, and he went aboard. The *Giraffe* went out and returned successfully, but from some cause (I never understood why) Herring failed to attract the attention of the land force and sent no message ashore. In the meantime the other steamer, the *Cornubia*, arrived in port, and Captain Alexander having been ordered elsewhere, and Lieutenant Doggett having been sent down from Richmond to take charge of the signal corps, General Whiting ordered a signal officer for the *Cornubia*, and I was detailed and sent to Wilmington to prepare the lights and report on board.

"We cleared the bar successfully, with Captain Burroughs in command, and C.C. Morse as pilot, and had a good voyage to St. George, Bermuda, where we unloaded our cargo of cotton and reloaded with supplies for the Southern Army. On our return trip we made the land fifty or sixty miles above Fort Fisher and coasted down to the inlet, our intention being to get near the land inside the blockading fleet, which was obliged to keep off a certain distance on account of shoal water. As well as I remember, when within fifteen to twenty miles of Fort Fisher, Captain Burroughs sent for me to come on the bridge, and asked if I had my lights ready, and if I thought I could send a message ashore, Pilot Morse in the meantime telling me that he would let me know when we were opposite the signal station on the land, where a constant watch was kept all night for our signal. We had not gone far when Morse told me we were opposite the post. We were feeling our way very slowly in the dark. I was put down on the deck, with the gangways open, my lights facing the land and a screen behind, when I was ordered to call the station. The officers and sailors were highly interested in the movement and crowded around to watch the proceedings. I had called but a few times when I was answered from the shore with a torch. I turned to Captain Burroughs and told him I had the attention of the land forces, and asked what message he wished to send. He replied as follows: 'Colonel Lamb, steamer *Cornubia*. Protect me. Burroughs.' I got the O.K. for the message from shore, and saw the corps on land call up one station after the other, and transmit my message down to Fort Fisher, miles ahead of us, and afterwards learned that General Whiting was notified by telegraph of the arrival of the *Cornubia* before she crossed the bar that night; and when we arrived at the fort we found Colonel Lamb down on the point with his Whitworth guns ready to protect us if necessary. The success of this attempt gave an impetus to the signal corps, and from that time every steamer that arrived applied to the Government for a signal officer before leaving port."

The name of the *Cornubia* was subsequently changed to *Lady Davis*, in honor of the wife of President Davis at Richmond, and Captain Gale, an officer of the old Navy who had gone over to the Confederacy, was placed in command. "About the 20th of December, 1863," Mr. Gregory adds, "we left Bermuda with a cargo for Wilmington in charge of Captain Gale, with Mr. Robert Grisson as pilot and myself as signal officer. We made land some miles above Wilmington, apparently through bad navigation, almost as far north as Cape Lookout, and when opposite Masonboro in coasting down we observed rockets going up directly ahead of us. We were running at full speed, when to our consternation rockets appeared quite near abreast of us; in fact we were apparently surrounded by cruisers. There was a hurried consultation on the bridge. I was at my post with my lights, waiting to be called, when the order was given to head for the beach and drive the ship high and dry. The blockaders were then cannonading us very heavily. When our good ship struck the beach she ploughed up the sand for a considerable distance, and keeled over on her side. The boats were lowered, and every man told to look out for himself, which I assure you we lost no time in doing, as we had scarcely left the ship before the enemy were boarding her on the opposite side and firing briskly with small arms. They followed us to the beach, and kept up a heavy fire from cannon and small arms for an hour.

We dodged about in the bulrushes as best we could, and made our way

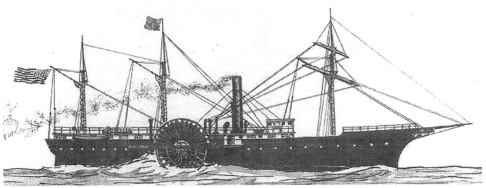

The **U.S.S. James Adger.**

toward the fort. Captain Thomas, acting chief officer, took ashore with him two fine chronometers, and selected me to carry one for him, but after beating around with them in the rushes for a mile or so, we became exhausted and had to throw them away. I have no doubt they are still lying in the rushes on the beach. We at last met a company of soldiers who protected and escorted us to the sound. We forded the sound and remained all night and were sent to Wilmington the next day, overland, by mule teams. I always thought it was a shame that the *Lady Davis* was lost, having no doubt we could have put to sea and escaped on the occasion referred to, although I was not informed as to the supply of coal on board.

"Captain Gale had been very sick the day before, and was too feeble to leave the ship, so remained on board and was captured and taken to Fort Warren. The *U.S.S. James Adger*, commanded by Capt. James Foster of Bloomington, Ind., had the good fortune to capture our ship, and hauled her off as a prize.

"After reaching Wilmington and supplying myself with clothing and a hat, I immediately went on board the steamer *Flora* with Captain Horner and made a successful run to Bermuda. The *Flora* was considered too slow and sent back to England. I then joined the *Index*, commanded by Captain Marshall, and made several successful voyages on her, but she too was condemned as too slow and was returned to Glasgow.

"I had a thrilling adventure on this ship on a homeward voyage, when, for the first time in all my experience, we made land opposite Bald Head Light on Frying Pan Shoals. As we were coming around to New Inlet we fell in with a Federal cruiser, so close when we discovered her that we could easily discern the maneuvers of the men on deck. She seemed to have anchors weighed, and was moving about and could easily have captured us, and we were at a loss to understand why she did not fire into us. Some of our people decided that she wished to secure us as a prize without injury, as she steamed alongside of us for miles and all at once put her helm hard down and went close under our stern and attempted to go between us and the shoals. I remember the remark of our pilot, Tom Grissom, to Captain Marshall: 'If she follows us on that course I will wreck her before we reach the inlet.'

"The cruiser had only steamed half a mile or so, when she suddenly passed from view, and in a few moments a rocket went up near where we last saw her, which was repeated at short intervals. After a few minutes, rockets could be seen going up from the whole squadron and there was evidently a great commotion among them on account of our pursuer, who seemed suddenly to have got into serious trouble. We passed through the inlet without further molestation, as the entire fleet had centered their attention upon the unfortunate cruiser which had suddenly gone down. When morning dawned, it revealed the Federal cruiser hard and fast on the reef, with the other vessels of the squadron working manfully to relieve her. Colonel Lamb went down to the extreme point with his Whitworth guns and opened fire on her. A month or so afterwards, while in Bermuda, I saw a spirited sketch of the whole affair in *Frank Leslie's Illustrated News*, giving an account of the wreck, and of an investigation of the conduct of the officers in charge. I think the vessel was the gun-boat *Petrel*.

"After the *Index* was sent back to Glasgow, Captain Marshall took charge of the steamer *Rouen* and I joined her as signal officer. We loaded our cargo and started for Wilmington, and on the third day out sighted a steamer about one o'clock p. m. This ship proved to be the *U.S.S. Keystone State*, which captured us after a hot chase of six hours. We were all transferred to the *Margaret and Jessie*, a former blockade runner which had been captured and utilized as a cruiser. We were taken to New York and confined in the Tombs Prison. Subsequently, all the officers and crew were discharged except four of us, and we were transferred to the Ludlow Street Jail for further investigation. After six weeks' imprisonment we succeeded in effecting our escape through the medium of English gold, after which we went down to East River and found an old barque loaded with staves and hay for St. Thomas. Each one of us gave the captain $25 in gold with the understanding that he would sail by St. George, Bermuda, and land us there. We reached this place after several weeks to find it devastated by yellow fever. Many personal friends died of this scourge, among whom was our lamented purser of the *Index*, Mr. Robert Williams, a well-known native of Wilmington, much beloved for his superior personal qualities.

"I then made one voyage in the *Owl*, which became famous under the command of Capt. John Newland Maffitt. After this I joined the new steel steamer *Susan Beirne*, commanded by Captain Martin, of which my old friend and shipmate James Sprunt was purser. After a very hazardous voyage in this ship, during which we weathered a fearful gale, and although we came very near foundering, we returned to Nassau to learn from Captain Maffitt of the steamer *Owl*, which had just arrived, that the last port of the Confederacy had been closed, and that the war was practically over.

"A small party of almost reckless Confederates, composed of our chief engineer, Mr. Lockhart; our second engineer, Mr. Carroll; our purser, Mr. James Sprunt, and the purser of another steamer in port, Maj. William Green, bought the steam launch belonging to our ship, a boat about forty feet in length and six feet breadth of beam, and made a perilous voyage by way of Green Turtle Cay to Cape Canaveral, Fla., where they landed in the surf after a two weeks' voyage, and proceeding on foot 175 miles to Ocala, Fla., succeeded in evading the Federal pickets and sentries at various points along the route and at last reached Wilmington, having occupied about two months on the way.

"I chose an easier and more agreeable route and proceeded via New York to visit some relatives in Indiana and returned later to North Carolina to find peace restored to our unhappy and desolated country."

Captain John Newland Maffitt

A mong that devoted band of United States Navy officers whose home and kindred were in the South at the outbreak of the War, and who resigned their commissions rather than aid in subjugating their native State, there was none braver than our own Capt. John Newland Maffitt, who, yielding to necessity, severed the strong ties of service under the old flag in which he had long distinguished himself, and relinquished not only a conspicuous position directly in line of speedy promotion to the rank of admiral, but sacrificed at the same time his entire fortune, which was invested in the North and which was confiscated shortly afterwards by the United States Government.

After the capture of the forts and the closing of the ports of Wilmington and Charleston in January, 1865, Maffitt, in command of the steamer *Owl* and unaware of the situation, ran into each port in quick succession, escaping from the fleet in each exploit as by a miracle, although under a heavy and destructive fire. While running out of Charleston Harbor when escape seemed impossible, his entire history of the cruise of the *Florida*, which he had so long successfully commanded, was, by an

Captain John Newland Maffitt.

unfortunate misunderstanding on the part of a subordinate, sent to the bottom of the sea, along with the Confederate mail and other valuable papers. Captain Maffitt, gifted with the pen of a ready writer, left many valuable accounts of his adventures, among them a story of naval life in the old service entitled "Nautilus," and a number of articles for the *Army and Navy Magazine* under the title "Reminiscences of the Confederate States Navy." His paper on the building of the ram *Albemarle* by Captain Cooke, and that gallant officer's subsequent attack upon the Federal fleet in Plymouth Sound, which is copied entire by Colonel Scharf in his history of the Confederate Navy, has been pronounced one of the finest descriptions of the Civil War. It was my privilege to be numbered among his personal friends from the time he honored me, a lad of seventeen years, with his recommendation for the appointment as purser of his own ship, the Confederate steamer *Lilian*, which was confirmed just before he gave up the command to take charge of the Confederate ram *Albemarle* at Plymouth; and this friendship was unbroken until the close of his eventful life, the sacrifices and services of which should ever be held in grateful remembrance by our Southern people.

In the year after my appointment to the *Lilian*, I had the misfortune to be captured at sea after an exciting chase of five hours by the Federal cruisers *Keystone State, Boston, Gettysburg*, and two others unknown, in which our ship was disabled under a heavy fire by shot below the water line, and was held a prisoner on board the *U.S.S. Keystone State*, whose commander, Captain Crosby, a regular in the old Navy, treated me most courteously. Upon the invitation of the paymaster, I messed with the superior officers in the wardroom, where I heard frequent bitter allusions to Captain Semmes and other prominent Confederates, but never a word of censure for the genial Maffitt, the mention of whose name would provoke a kindly and amused smile as some of his pranks in the old times would be recalled by those who had not learned to regard him as a foe.

The following passages, taken from Admiral Porter's *Naval History of the Civil War*, confirm the personal observations of the writer with reference to Maffitt's reputation in the old Navy:

"Maffitt was a different man from Semmes. A thorough master of his profession, and possessed of all the qualities that make a favorite naval commander, he became a successful raider of the sea; but he made no enemies among those officers who had once known him and who now missed his genial humor in their messes. He was a veritable rover, but was never inhumane to those whom the fortunes of war threw into his hands, and he made himself as pleasant while emptying a ship of her cargo and then scuttling her, as Claude Duval when robbing a man of his purse or borrowing his watch from his pocket."

Porter then describes in almost flattering terms Maffitt's superior skill and daring in fitting out the *Florida* under most adverse conditions, and then by way of explantion says:

"It may appear to the reader that we have exhibited more sympathy for Commander Maffitt and given him more credit than he deserved; it must be remembered that we are endeavoring to write a naval history of the war, and not a partisan work. This officer, it is true, had gone from under the flag we venerate to fight against it; but we know it was a sore trial for him to leave the service to which he was attached and that he believed he was doing his duty in following the fortunes of his State, and had the courage to follow his convictions. He did not leave the U.S. Navy with any bitterness, and when the troubles were all over, he accepted the situation gracefully. What we are going to state of him shows that he was capable of the greatest heroism, and that, though he was on the side of the enemy, his courage and skill were worthy of praise."

He then recounts the wonderful story of Maffitt's perilous run through Commander Preble's fleet in broad daylight, with a crew decimated by yellow fever, and he himself scarcely able to stand from its prostrating effects.

"The *Florida* approached rapidly, her smoke pipes vomiting forth volumes of black smoke and a high press of steam escaping from her steam pipe. As she came within hailing distance, the Federal commander ordered her to heave to, but Maffitt still sped on, having sent all his men below, except the man at the wheel, and returned to reply to the hail. Preble then fired a shot ahead of the *Florida*, still supposing her to be some saucy Englishman disposed to try what liberties he could take, though the absence of men on deck should have excited suspicion. He hesitated, however, and hesitation lost him a prize and the honor of capturing one of the Confederate scourges of the ocean. Preble had his crew at quarters, however, and as soon as he saw that the stranger was passing him he opened his broadside upon her and the other two blockaders did the same. But the first shots were aimed too high, and the *Florida* sped on toward the bar, her feeble crew forgetting their sickness and heaping coal upon the furnace fires with all possible rapidity. Every man was working for his life, while the captain stood amid the storm of shot and shell perfectly unmoved, keenly watching the marks for entering the port and wondering to himself what his chances were for getting in.

"During the whole war there was not a more exciting adventure than this escape of the *Florida* into Mobile Bay. The gallant manner in which it was conducted excited great admiration, even among the men who were responsible for permitting it. We do not suppose that there was ever a case where a man, under all the attending circumstances, displayed more energy or more bravery.

The **C.S.S. Florida.**

"And so the *Florida* was allowed to go on her way without molestation, and Maffitt was enabled to commence that career on the high seas which has made his name one of the notable ones of the war. He lighted the seas wherever he passed along, and committed such havoc among American merchantmen, that, if possible, he was even more dreaded than Semmes. We have only to say that his being permitted to escape into Mobile Bay and then to get out again was the greatest example of blundering committed throughout the war. Every officer who knew Maffitt was certain that he would attempt to get out of Mobile, and we are forced to say that those who permitted his escape are responsible for the terrible consequences of their want of vigilance and energy."

Preble's failure to sink the *Florida*—for nothing else would have stopped Maffitt—brought him into disgrace with the Navy Department, although he proved in his report of the affair that every means at his command had been used to intercept the bold Confederate, and shortly afterwards the Secretary of the Navy, supported by a majority of naval officers, recommended the dismissal of Commodore Preble from the Navy, which was carried into effect September 20, 1863.

Preble repeatedly demanded an investigation, which was refused, but he ultimately got his case before Congress and was restored to the list February 21, 1864, with the grade of rear admiral.

At the close of the war Captain Maffitt was summoned by a court of inquiry demanded by Preble to testify as to the facts of his exploit in entering Mobile Bay, in which he said:

"I can vouch for his (Preble's) promptness and destructive energy on the occasion of my entering Mobile Bay. The superior speed of the *Florida* alone saved her from destruction, though not from a frightful mauling. We were torn to pieces—one man's head taken off and eleven wounded; boats, standing and running rigging shot away, also fore gaff. Four shells struck our hull and had the one (9-inch) that grazed our boiler and entered the berth deck, killing one and wounding two, exploded every man belonging to the steamer would have been killed, as I had only the officers on deck until about to cross the bar, when I made some sail, and one man was wounded in the rigging. We had about 1,400 shrapnel shots in our hull, and our masts were pitted like a case of smallpox. The damage done her was so great that we did not get to sea again for over three months."

The last voyage of Captain Maffitt was made on the *Owl*, which he boarded at Wilmington the 21st of December, 1864, receiving her cargo of

750 bales of cotton. With three other blockade runners in company he started for the bar. He escaped the Federal sentinels "without the loss of a rope yarn," though one of his companions came to grief through an accident to machinery. Their destination was St. George, Bermuda, which they reached in safety, finding several steamers loaded and anxiously awaiting news from the Federal expedition under General Butler against Fort Fisher. Through a Halifax steamer the Northern papers apprised them of the failure of the expedition, and in company with six other steamers and many gallant spirits, the *Owl* started on her return to Dixie, all cheered by the joyful news.

In the meantime another expedition against Fort Fisher had been fitted out under General Terry and Admiral Porter, which had been successful, and the river was in possession of the Federals.

Communicating with Lockwood's Folly, where they reported all quiet and Fisher intact, Captain Maffitt steamed for the Cape Fear. At eight o'clock it was high water on the bar, and the moon would not rise before eleven. Approaching the channel, he was surprised to see but one sentinel guarding the entrance. Eluding him, he passed in. Some apprehension was excited by a conflagration at Bald Head and no response to his signals, but as Fort Caswell looked natural and quiet, he decided to anchor off the fort wharf. He was immediately interviewed by the chief of ordnance and artillery, E.S. Martin, and another officer, who informed him of the state of affairs, and that the train was already laid for the blowing up of Fort Caswell. Gunboats were approaching, and in great distress Captain Maffitt hastily departed. A solitary blockader pursued him furiously for some time, and far at sea he heard the explosion that announced the fate of Caswell. As his cargo was important and much needed, Captain Maffitt determined to make an effort to enter the port of Charleston, although he had been informed that it was more closely guarded than ever before.

Many attempts were made to overhaul his vessel as he made his way into the harbor, but it was only necessary to stir up the fire draft a bit to start off with truly admirable speed that enabled him to outdistance his pursuers. Anticipating a trying night and the bare possibility of capture, the captain had two bags slung and suspended over the quarter by a stout line. In these bags were placed the Government mail not yet delivered, all private correspondence and the captain's war journal in which was the cruise of the *Florida.* An intelligent quartermaster was instructed to stand by the bags with a hatchet, and to cut them adrift the moment capture became inevitable.

The following is a description of what happened in Captain Maffitt's own words:

"When on the western tail end of Rattlesnake Shoal, we encountered streaks of mist and fog that enveloped stars and everything for a few moments, when it would become quite clear again. Running cautiously in one of these obscurations, a sudden lift in the haze disclosed that we were about to run into an anchored blockader. We had bare room with a hard-a-port helm to avoid him some fifteen or twenty feet, when their officer on deck called out: 'Heave to, or I'll sink you.' The order was unnoticed, and we received his entire broadside, which cut away turtleback, perforated forecastle, and tore up bulwarks in front of our engine room, wounding twelve men, some severely, some slightly. The quartermaster stationed by the mail bags was so convinced that we were captured that he instantly used his hatchet, and sent them, well moored, to the bottom. Hence my meager account of the cruise of the *Florida.* Rockets were fired as we passed swiftly out of his range of sight, and Drummond lights lit up the animated surroundings of a swarm of blockaders, who commenced an indiscriminate discharge of artillery. We could not understand the reason of this bombardment, and as we picked our way out of the melee, concluded that several blockade runners must have been discovered feeling their way into Charleston.

"After the war, in conversing with the officer commanding on that occasion, he said that a number of the steamers of the blockade were commanded by inexperienced volunteer officers, who were sometimes overzealous and excitable, and hearing the gunboats firing into me, and seeing her rockets and signal lights, they thought that innumerable blockade runners were forcing a passage into the harbor, hence the indiscriminate discharge of artillery, which was attended with unfortunate results to them. This was my last belligerent association with blockade running. Entering the harbor of Charleston, and finding it in the possession of the Federals, I promptly checked progress and retreated. The last order issued by the Navy Department, when all hope for the cause had departed, was for me to deliver the *Owl* to Frazier, Trenholme & Co., in Liverpool, which I accordingly did."

Captain Maffit and the Consul

The following story was told me by the veteran blockade runner George C. McDougal:

"When the Yankees ran the *Kate* out of New Smyrna, Fla., we had to run across light and leave Capt. Thomas Lockwood, who had gone to Charleston, behind. The command devolved on Mr. Carlin, first officer. We got the ship into Nassau Saturday night. On the following day, Sunday, the British mail steamer appeared off Nassau with the new Governor of the Bahamas on board, but owing to a heavy sea on the bar she could not cross, and accordingly ran down to the west end of the island and to smoother water in order to land the Governor. During the day a number of prominent inhabitants of Nassau came aboard the *Kate* and asked if the captain would go down to the west end and bring the Governor up. Captain Carlin told them that they were quite welcome to the ship if she could be got ready in time, which would depend upon the chief engineer. He immediately consulted with me and we decided that as the people of Nassau had been very kind to us, the *Kate* being a favorite, we would try to accommodate them at once. As we had arrived after midnight on Saturday, and, not wishing to work on Sunday, we had not blown the boilers out. The water was hot, and I told the captain I would be ready in an hour's time or less. I started the fires immediately and in a few minutes the committee went on shore to gather their friends and to send off refreshments. In a short time gunboats began to crowd alongside with the aforesaid refreshments, both solid and liquid, the latter as usual predominating in the shape of cases of champagne, brandy, etc.

"When the guests were all on board we hove up the anchor and faced the bar. A tremendous sea was running, and at times our topgallant forecastle was under water. We worked out, however, and hauled down the coast for the west end. In a short time the refreshments began to work on the company, especially on the mate. Captain Carlin being afraid that the small anchor would not hold the ship, ordered the mate to get the large anchor from between decks to the gangway, carry the chain from the hawse pipe along the side of the ship by tricing lines and shackle it to the anchor. I noticed that the mate was almost incapable from the aforesaid refreshments, and I said to him, 'You will lose that anchor,' to which he replied, 'I know what I am about.' Presently the ship took a roll down into the trough of the sea, and overboard went the anchor. When it struck bottom the ship was going twelve or fourteen miles an hour and the sudden jerk started the chain around the windlass, and the way that seventy fathoms of chain flew around the windlass and out of the hawse pipe made the fire fly. It looked as if half a dozen flashes of lightning were playing hide and seek between the decks. With a crack like a pistol shot the weather bitting parted and the end of the chain went out of the hawse pipe to look for the anchor.

"We soon made the bay at the west end and ran alongside the mail steamer and let go our anchor, but found to our disappointment that the

Governor had gone to town in a carriage sent for him by the officials. After spending a pleasant hour in exchanging visits between the officers of the two steamers, our guests in the meantime partaking of refreshments, we hove up the anchor and started back toward Nassau.

"Among our passengers was the gallant Capt. John N. Maffitt, who was then waiting at Nassau to get the *Oreto*, afterwards named the *Florida*, out of irons. We had also Captain Whiting, the American consul at Nassau, who asked permission to go down to the steamer to get his dispatches, which was not denied him, although this man was greatly disliked not only by Confederate sympathizers but by the natives, having, as the Irishman said, winning ways to make everybody hate him. During the run back the consul, overcome by his numerous potations, lay down with his dispatches and was soon asleep. When we aroused him at our destination the dispatches were missing, whereupon he accused Maffitt of stealing them, resulting in a grand row all round. The dispatches were restored to him on the following day, their disappearance being caused by a practical joke on the part of the Confederates. We delivered our passengers in a very shaky condition.

"On Monday morning, having turned out bright and early to start work, our attention was attracted to the shore by a noisy and excited group of negroes gathered around the flagstaff of the American consul, gesticulating and pointing to the top of the flag-staff, from which, to my astonishment, was flying a brand new Confederate flag. It soon appeared that some one, said to be a Confederate sympathizer, and whom every one believed to be Maffitt, who was always ready for a joke, had climbed the flagstaff during the night, carrying up with him a Confederate flag and a bucket of slush. The halyards were first unrove, next the Confederate flag was nailed to the staff, and last of all as the joker descended, he slushed the staff all the way to the ground, making it impossible for any one to ascend to remove the ensign which was so hateful to our friend the consul. When Whiting came down to the consulate after breakfast and took in the situation, he performed a war dance around that pole which was one of the most interesting spectacles ever witnessed by the Confederates in Nassau. He then employed a number of Her Majesty's colored subjects with cans of concentrated lye to remove the slush, and, after great difficulty, one of them succeeded in reaching the top of the staff and removed the Confederate flag, replacing the halyards as before; but this was not the last of it. On the following morning a United States man-of-war appeared off the harbor, and when the consul in full official rig took his seat in the stern of his gig he found on reaching the cruiser that he was hard and fast by the nether extremities, some North Carolina tar having been previously applied by the aforesaid Confederate sympathizer to the seat of his gig. Of course these annoyances created a great deal of feeling, and a down-east shipmaster, desiring to show his spite, made a fool of himself by hoisting the American flag over the British flag, the latter being union down, intending it as an insult, of course, which was immediately noticed on shore, and in a short time several thousand shouting, howling British negroes were lining the water front looking for boats and threatening to drown the American captain who had taken such a liberty with their beloved flag. Before they could carry out their purpose, however, a man-of-war's launch shot out from the British gunboat *Bulldog* with a file of marines, and, boarding the brig, ordered the flags hauled down and the English flag detached, took the captain in the launch and pulled to the government wharf and immediately shoved him into the calaboose, from which confinement he was not released until the next day, with the admonition that if he remained on board his ship he would have no need of a surgeon. He took the hint and was seen no more on shore.

"On Thursday we were bound for the northwest channel with our regulation cargo of 1,000 barrels of gunpowder and arms and accouterments for 10,000 men. We ran into Charleston on Saturday night and on Sunday morning the Confederate quartermaster pressed every horse and dray in Charleston to haul the cargo to the railroad station. The congregations of the churches along Meeting and King Streets probably derived very little benefit from the sermons delivered that sacred day, as the roar of the drays and wagons was incessant all day Sunday and Sunday night. As fast as a train was loaded it was started out for Johnston's army, and a conductor of a train told me afterwards that the soldiers broke open the cases of rifles on the cars and distributed the firearms and accouterments from the car doors. It may be said that the *Kate* was a most important factor in the battle of Shiloh. Johnston's army was a mass of undisciplined men with single and double barrel shotguns, old time rifles, and anything else in the way of firearms that they could bring from home. They had nothing suitable to fight with. The three cargoes of war stores, therefore, carried in by the *Kate*, one by the *Mary Celeste* to Smyrna and the fourth cargo carried by the *Kate* into Charleston, actually equipped Johnston's army, immediately after which came the battle of Shiloh. One thousand barrels of gunpowder was a dangerous shipment to run through the Federal blockade, and it was a great relief to us when the Confederacy established powder mills in Georgia, and our powder cargoes were changed to niter for the mills."

Captain John Wilkinson

One of the most intelligent and successful commanders of the blockade-running fleet was Capt. John Wilkinson, who entered the United States Navy as a midshipman in 1837, and, after an honorable and distinguished career, tendered his services upon the secession of his native State, Virginia, to the Confederacy.

Having received a commission in the Confederate States Navy, he served in various responsible positions until ordered upon special service in command of the Confederate States steamer *R.E. Lee*.

In his interesting book entitled *Narrative of a Blockade Runner*, speaking of the citizens of Virginia who resigned their commissions in the old service, he says:

"They were compelled to choose whether they would aid in subjugating their State or in defending it against invasion; for it was already evident that coercion would be used by the General Government, and that war was inevitable. In reply to the accusation of perjury in breaking their oath of allegiance, since brought against the officers of the Army and Navy who resigned their commissions to render aid to the South, it need only be stated that, in their belief, the resignation of their commissions absolved

Captain John Wilkinson.

them from any special obligation. They then occupied the same position toward the Government as other classes of citizens. But this charge was never brought against them till the war was ended. The resignation of their commissions was accepted when their purpose was well known. As to the charge of ingratitude, they reply, their respective States had contributed their full share toward the expenses of the General Government, acting as their disbursing agent, and when these States withdrew from the Union their citizens belonging to the two branches of the public service did not, and do not, consider themselves amenable to this charge for abandoning their official positions to cast their lot with their kindred and friends. But yielding as they did to necessity, it was, nevertheless, a painful act to separate themselves from companions with whom they had been long and intimately associated, and from the flag under which they had been proud to serve."

With reference to his experience in blockade running at Wilmington Captain Wilkinson continues:

"The natural advantages of Wilmington for blockade running were very great, chiefly owing to the fact that there were two separate and distinct approaches to Cape Fear River; i.e., either by New Inlet, to the north of Smith's Island, or by the Western Bar to the south of it. This island is ten or eleven miles in length; but the Frying Pan Shoals extend ten or twelve miles farther south, making the distance by sea between the two bars thirty miles or more, although the direct distance between them is only six or seven miles. From Smithville (now Southport), a little village nearly equidistant from either bar, both blockading fleets could be distinctly seen, and the outward-bound blockade runners could take their choice through which of them to run the gauntlet. The inwardbound blockade runners, too, were guided by circumstances of wind and weather, selecting that bar over which they could cross after they had passed the Gulf Stream, and shaping their course accordingly. The approaches to both bars were clear of danger with the single exception of the 'Lump,' before mentioned; and so regular are the soundings that the shore can be coasted for miles within a stone's throw of the breakers.

"These facts explain why the United States fleet was unable wholly to stop blockade running. It was, indeed, impossible to do so; the result to the very close of the war proves this assertion, for, in spite of the vigilance of the fleet, many blockade runners were afloat when Fort Fisher was captured. In truth the passage through the fleet was little dreaded; for although the blockade runner might receive a shot or two, she was rarely disabled; and in proportion to the increase of the fleet the greater would be the danger, we knew, of their firing into each other. As the boys before the deluge used to say, they would be very apt to 'miss the cow and kill the calf.' The chief danger was upon the open sea, many of the light cruisers having great speed. As soon as one of them discovered a blockade runner during daylight, she would attract other cruisers in the vicinity by sending up a dense column of smoke, visible for many miles in clear weather. A cordon of fast steamers stationed ten or fifteen miles apart, inside the Gulf Stream, and in the course from Nassau and Bermuda to Wilmington and Charleston, would have been more effectual in stopping blockade running than the whole United States Navy concentrated off those ports; and it was unaccountable to us why such

Capt. Wilkinson's ship, the blockade-runner **Robert E. Lee.** *After it was captured it became the* **U.S.S. Fort Donelson.**

a plan did not occur to good Mr. Welles; but it was not our place to suggest it. I have no doubt, however, that the fraternity to which I then belonged would have unanimously voted thanks and a service of plate to the Honorable Secretary of the United States Navy for this oversight. I say *inside the Gulf Stream*, because every experienced captain of a blockade runner made a point to cross the stream early enough in the afternoon, if possible, to establish the ship's position by chronometer, so as to escape the influence of that current upon his dead reckoning. The lead always gave indication of our distance from the land, but not, of course, of our position; and the numerous salt works along the coast, where evaporation was produced by fire, and which were at work night and day, were visible long before the low coast could be seen. Occasionally the whole inward voyage would be made under adverse conditions. Cloudy, thick weather and heavy gales would prevail so as to prevent any solar or lunar observations, and reduce the dead reckoning to mere guesswork. In these cases the nautical knowledge and judgment of the captain would be taxed to the utmost. The current of the Gulf Stream varies in velocity and (within certain limits) in direction; and the stream itself, almost as well defined as a river within its banks under ordinary circumstances, is impelled by a strong gale toward the direction in which the wind is blowing, overflowing its banks, as it were. The countercurrent, too, inside of the Gulf Stream, is much influenced by the prevailing winds. Upon one occasion while in command of the *R.E. Lee*, formerly the Clyde-built iron steamer *Giraffe*, we had experienced very heavy and thick weather, and had crossed the stream and struck soundings about midday. The weather then clearing, so that we could obtain an altitude near meridian, we found ourselves at least forty miles north of our supposed position, and near the shoals which extend in a southerly direction off Cape Lookout. It would be more perilous to run out to sea than to continue on our course, for we had passed through the offshore line of blockaders, and the sky had become perfectly clear. I determined to personate a transport bound to Beaufort, which was in the possession of the United States forces and the coaling station of the fleet blockading Wilmington. The risk of detection was not very great, for many of the captured blockade runners were used as transports and dispatch vessels. Shaping our course for Beaufort and slowing down as if we were in no haste to get there, we passed several vessels, showing United States colors to them all. Just as we were crossing through the ripple of shallow water off the 'tail' of the shoals, we dipped our colors to a sloop of war which passed three or four miles to the south of us. The courtesy was promptly responded to, but I have no doubt her captain thought me a lubberly and careless seaman to shave the shoals so closely. We stopped the engines when no vessel was in sight, and I was relieved of a heavy burden of anxiety as the sun sank below the horizon, and the course was shaped at full speed for Masonboro Inlet.

"The staid old town of Wilmington was turned 'topsy turvey' during the war. Here resorted the speculators from all parts of the South to attend the weekly auctions of imported cargoes; and the town was infested with rogues and desperadoes, who made a livelihood by robbery and murder. It was unsafe to venture into the suburbs at night, and even in daylight there were frequent conflicts in the public streets between the crews of the steamers in port and the soldiers stationed in the town, in which knives and pistols would be freely used; and not unfrequently a dead body would rise to the surface of the water in one of the docks with marks of violence upon it. The civil authorities were powerless to prevent crime. *'Inter arma silent leges!'* The agents and employees of different blockade-running companies lived in magnificent style, paying a king's ransom (in Confederate money) for their household expenses, and nearly monopolizing the supplies in the country market. Toward the end of the war, indeed, fresh provisions were almost beyond the reach of everyone. Our family servant, newly arrived from the country in Virginia, would sometimes return from market with an empty basket, having flatly refused to pay what he called 'such nonsense prices' for a bit of fresh beef, or a handful of vegetables. A quarter of lamb at the time of which I now write, sold for $100, a pound of tea for $500. Confederate money which in September, 1861, was nearly equal to specie in value, had declined in September, 1862, to 225; in the same month, in 1863, to 400, and before September, 1864, to 2,000!

"Many of the permanent residents of the town had gone into the country, letting their houses at enormous prices; those who were compelled to remain kept themselves much secluded, the ladies rarely being seen upon the more public streets. Many of the fast young officers belonging to the Army would get an occasional leave to come to Wilmington, and would live at free quarters on board the blockade runners or at one of the numerous bachelor halls ashore.

"The convalescent soldiers from the Virginia hospitals were sent by the route through Wilmington to their homes in the South. The ladies of the town were organized by Mrs. deRosset into a society for the purpose of ministering to the wants of these poor sufferers, the trains which carried them stopping an hour or two at the depot, that their wounds might be dressed and food and medicine supplied to them. These self-sacrificing, heroic women patiently and faithfully performed the offices of hospital nurses.

"Liberal contributions were made by companies and individuals to this society, and the long tables at the depot were spread with delicacies for the sick to be found nowhere else in the Confederacy. The remains of the meals were carried by the ladies to a camp of mere boys—home guards outside of the town. Some of these children were scarcely able to carry a musket and were altogether unable to endure the exposure and fatigue of field service; and they suffered fearfully from measles and typhoid fever. General Grant used a strong figure of speech when he asserted that 'the cradle and the grave were robbed to recruit the Confederate armies.' The fact of a fearful drain upon the population was scarcely exaggerated, but with this difference in the metaphor, that those who were verging upon both the cradle and the grave shared the hardships and dangers of war with equal self-devotion to the cause. It is true that a class of heartless speculators infested the country, who profited by the scarcity of all sorts of supplies, but it makes the self-sacrifice of the mass of the Southern people more conspicuous, and no State made more liberal voluntary contributions to the armies or furnished better soldiers than North Carolina.

"On the opposite side of the river from Wilmington, on a low marshy flat, were erected the steam cotton presses, and there the blockade runners took in their cargoes. Sentries were posted on the wharves day and night to prevent deserters from getting aboard and stowing themselves away; and the additional precaution of fumigating outwardbound steamers at Smithville was adopted, but in spite of this vigilance, many persons succeeded in getting a free passage aboard. These deserters, or 'stowaways,' were in most instances sheltered by one or more of the crew, in which event they kept their places of concealment until the steamer had arrived at her port of destination, when they would profit by the first opportunity to leave the vessel undiscovered. A small bribe would tempt the average blockade-running sailor to connive at this means of escape. The impecunious deserter fared more hardly and would usually be forced by hunger or thirst to emerge from his hiding place while the steamer was on the outward voyage. A cruel device employed by one of the captains effectually put a stop, I believe, certainly a check, to the escape of this class of 'stowaways.' He turned three

Mound Battery, near the New Inlet entrance to the Cape Fear River.

or four of them adrift in the Gulf Stream in an open boat with a pair of oars and a few days' allowance of bread and water."

Colonel Scharf, writing of the Confederate States Navy, mentions the shore lights: "At the beginning of the war," he says, "nearly all the lights along the Southern coast had been discontinued, the apparatus being removed to places of safety. In 1864 it was deemed expedient to re-establish the light on Smith's Island, which had been discontinued ever since the beginning of hostilities, and to erect a structure for a light on the 'Mound.' The 'Mound' was an artificial one, erected by Colonel Lamb, who commanded Fort Fisher." Captain Wilkinson says of the "Mound" and the range lights: "Two heavy guns were mounted upon it, and it eventually became a site for a light, and very serviceable for blockade runners; but even at this period it was an excellent landmark. Joined by a long, low isthmus of sand with the higher mainland, its regular conical shape enabled the blockade runners easily to identify it from the offing; and in clear weather, it showed plain and distinct against the sky at night. I believe the military men used to laugh slyly at the colonel for undertaking its erection, predicting that it would not stand; but the result showed the contrary; and whatever difference of opinion may have existed with regard to its value as a military position, there can be but one as to its utility to the blockade runners, for it was not a landmark alone, along this monotonous coast, but one of the range lights for crossing New Inlet Bar was placed on it. Seamen will appreciate at its full value this advantage; but it may be stated for the benefit of the unprofessional reader, that while the compass bearing of an object does not enable a pilot to steer a vessel with sufficient accuracy through a narrow channel, range lights answer the purpose completely. These lights were only set after signals had been exchanged between the blockade runner and the shore station, and were removed immediately after the vessel had entered the river. The range lights were changed as circumstances required; for the New Inlet Channel itself was and is constantly changing, being materially affected both in depth of water and in its course by a heavy gale of wind or a severe freshet in Cape Fear River."

A Normal Blockading Experience

Probably one of the quickest and most uneventful voyages made during the war in running the blockade was that made by Capt. C.G. Smith, of Southport. The following story on the blockade was told by Captain Smith, and is published to show the contrast between what some of the blockade runners had to undergo and how easy it was at other times to make the round trip without hindrance or adventure:

"On a delightful day, about the first of May, 1863, I left Nassau as pilot on the fine side-wheel steamer *Margaret and Jessie*, Captain Wilson in command.

"The *Margaret and Jessie* was at that time regarded as one of the fastest steamers. Of about 800 tons, this steamer when in ballast could make fifteen miles an hour, but of course she was usually loaded down, therefore seldom doing better than ten knots while running the blockade.

"Passing out from Nassau with a general cargo of goods, bound for Wilmington, N.C., the first twenty-four hours were passed without incident, the steamer making a good passage, until a gale from the northeast met us, which lasted till noon of the third day out.

"When the wind had lessened somewhat, Captain Wilson came to me and asked what point of land I wanted to make, to which I replied that I intended to run in at the Western Bar of the Cape Fear. Finding it an impossibility on account of the weather to make the Western Bar before daylight, I made for Masonboro and came in at New Inlet, anchoring abreast of the mound battery which guarded this approach at about 11 o'clock at night, and at daylight, with a fair tide, ran up to Wilmington.

"Nothing in the shape of a blockader disturbed our voyage. At one time a steamer was seen east-southeast of us, but paid no attention to us. When at Masonboro, one of the blockading squadron went to the southeastward of us, but being under the lee of the land she could not make us out.

"After laying up in Wilmington about ten days, discharging our cargo and taking on a load of cotton, we quietly dropped down the river one morning, and, anchoring in five-fathom hole, waited until night, when we passed out of New Inlet, bound for Nassau.

"The return trip was made without incident of any kind, the weather was fine, not a vessel of any description could be seen on the voyage; and in fifty-two hours from the time of leaving the Cape Fear, we were safe at the dock at Nassau, discharging our cargo, making one of the quickest and safest passages ever made by any of the blockade runners."

Joseph Fry

Captain Joseph Fry

In the year 1841, a winsome, honest lad who had determined to join the Navy of his country, and who had been thwarted in his purpose by friends at home, made his way alone from Florida to Washington and demanded his right to speak to the President, which was not denied him.

Mr. Tyler was so pleased by the youthful manliness of the little chap, who was only eight years old, that he invited him to dine at the White House on the following day. The young Floridian was the observed of all observers; members of the Cabinet and their wives, members of Congress and officers of the Navy had heard of the little lad's story, and all united in espousing his patriotic cause.

The President, won by his ardor as well as by his gentlemanly and modest behavior, granted the boy's request and immediately signed his warrant as a midshipman in the United States Navy.

The subsequent record of Capt. Joseph Fry, the Christian gentleman, the gallant sailor, the humane commander, the chivalrous soldier, is known

to readers of American history. Of heroic mould and dignified address, he
was

> "A combination and a form indeed,
> Where every god did seem to set his seal
> To give the world assurance of a man."

When the Civil War came, it found him among the most beloved and
honored officers in the service. The trial of his faith was bitter but brief. He
could not fight against his home and loved ones, much as he honored the

Agnes E. Fry.

flag which he had so long and
faithfully cherished. He was a
Southerner, and with many pangs of
sincere regret he went with his
native State for weal or woe.

His personal bravery during the
war was wonderful; he never
performed deeds of valor under
temporary excitement, but acted
with such coolness and daring as to
command the admiration of
superiors and inferiors alike. He was
severely wounded at the battle of
White River, and while on sick
leave was ordered, at his own
request, to command the
Confederate blockade runner
Eugenie, upon which the writer
made a voyage.

On one occasion the *Eugenie*
grounded outside of Fort Fisher while trying to run through the fleet in
daylight. The ship was loaded with gunpowder, the Federal fleet was firing
upon her, the risk of immediate death and destruction to crew and ship was
overwhelming. Fry was ordered by Colonel Lamb to abandon the vessel and
save his crew from death by explosion. He accordingly told all who wished
to go to do so, but as for himself, he would stand by the ship and try to save
the powder, which was greatly needed by the Confederate Government.
Several boatloads of his men retreated to the fort; a few remained with Fry,
the enemy's shells flying thick and fast around them. In the face of this great

danger, Fry lightened his ship, and upon the swelling tide brought vessel and cargo safely in.

Later on he commanded the steamer *Agnes E. Fry*, named in honor of his devoted wife. In this ship he made three successful voyages, after which she was unfortunately run ashore by her pilot and lies not far distant from the *Virginius*. Captain Fry was then placed in active service during the remainder of the war in command of the Confederate gunboat *Morgan* and was highly complimented by his general, Dabney H. Maury, for conspicuous bravery in action.

After the war his fortunes underwent many changes. Several undertakings met with varying success or failure. At last, he went to New York in July, 1873, where he hoped to secure employment in command of an ocean steamer. There he was introduced to General Quesada, agent of the Cuban Republic, who offered him the command of the steamer *Virginius*, then lying in the harbor of Kingston, Jamaica. He accepted the offer, and received a month's pay in advance, $150, two-thirds of which he sent to his needy family, and reserved the remainder for his personal outfit. The *Virginius*, originally named *Virgin*, was built in Scotland in 1864 and was specially designed for a blockade runner in the Confederate service. She made several successful trips between Havana and Mobile. Being shut up in the latter port, she was used by the Confederates as a dispatch and transport steamer. For a time after the war she was used by the Federal Government in the United States Revenue Service, but proving unsatisfactory, owing to her great consumption of coal, was sold at public auction by the United States

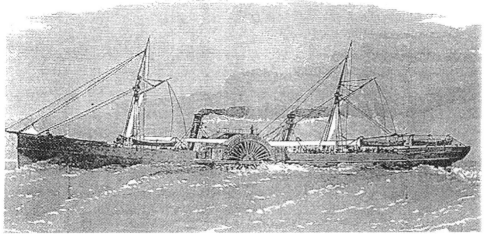

*The **Virginius** as drawn by a Cuban naval officer, after the American Civil War.*

The Spanish ship* Tornado, *which captured Captain Fry in international waters.

Treasury Department to an American firm. The owners in 1870 took out American papers in legal form and cleared her for Venezuela. From that time she was used in carrying volunteers and supplies to Cuba; and while engaged in this business under the American flag, recognized by American consuls as an American vessel, she was overhauled at sea on the 31st of October, 1873, by the Spanish man-of-war *Tornado* and declared a prize to the Spanish Government. Fry never dreamed of greater danger; he occupied the same position he had assumed while running the Federal blockade and the same as in the recent cases of the *Commodore* and the *Bermuda*. He was a merchantman, carried no guns, made no armed resistance, and flew the American flag. Notwithstanding all this, a drumhead court martial was held on board the *Tornado* and on the second day afterwards the unfortunate victims were condemned as pirates and sentenced to immediate execution at Santiago de Cuba, where the Spanish warship had arrived. Even then Captain Fry and his crew, who were nearly all Americans, expected a release through the intervention of the United States authorities. Vain hope! The American consul was absent; the vice-consul did what he could in vain; the Home Government was silent; the British consul protested, but without avail, and the butchery of these brave men began. We read from the newspaper accounts of the dreadful scene as the victims were ranged facing a wall. Captain Fry asked for a glass of water, which was given him by the friendly hand of one of his own race. He then walked with firm, unfaltering steps to the place assigned him, and calmly awaited the volley which ended his noble life.

A touching incident occurred on the march to execution. When the brave man passed the American Consulate, he gravely saluted the bare pole which should have borne the flag, once and again so dear to his heart, but which had failed him in his extremity.

Although the firing party was only ten feet away, says the published account, Fry was the only one killed outright. Then ensued a horrible scene. "The Spanish butchers advanced to where the wounded men lay, writhing and moaning in agony, and placing the muzzles of their guns in the mouths of their victims, shattered their heads into fragments. Others were stabbed to death with knives and swords."

Fifty-three victims had suffered death, ninety-three more were made ready for execution; the bloody work was to be resumed, when an unlookedfor intervention came. The news had reached Jamaica, and it found in the harbor the British man-of-war *Niobe* under command of Capt. Sir Lambton Lorraine, who, true to his Anglo-Saxon instincts, needed no orders to speed to the rescue. Leaving in such haste that many of his men were left behind, he steamed with forced draft to Santiago. Before the anchor reached the bottom of the harbor the *Niobe's* drums had beat to quarters and the well-trained gunners were at their stations.

Commander Lorraine ignored the customary formalities; precious lives were trembling in the balance; moments were vital. Before the Spanish

The execution of the **Virginius'** *crew at Santiago de Cuba.*

*The **H.M.S. Niobe**, whose timely arrival saved the lives of the remaining crew.*

general was made aware of his arrival, Lorraine stood before him and demanded that the execution be stayed. To Burriel's unsatisfactory response the brave commander returned answer that in the absence of an American man-of-war he would protect the interest of the Americans. Still the Spaniard hesitated; he had tasted human blood, but his thirst was not satisfied. Again the gallant Britisher demanded an unequivocal answer, and, report says, confirmed it by a threat that he would bombard the town, as he had in Honduras for the protection of the Anglo-Saxon. His prompt, decisive action arrested the bloody work, and eventually saved the lives of the remainder of the crew of the *Virginius*.

On his return to England some months later, Sir Lambton was detained some days in New York. The city authorities, animated by his gallant conduct, tendered him a public reception, which was modestly declined. Virginia City, Nev., desiring to testify its appreciation of his noble humanity, forwarded to him a fourteen-pound brick of solid silver, upon which was inscribed his name and the incident, with the legend "Blood is thicker than water," signifying also in Western eulogy "You're a brick."

A tardy recognition of the rights of American possession was made later by the Spanish Government, and the *Virginius* was delivered to an American man-of-war. While towing the unfortunate craft off Cape Fear and bound for a Northern port, the *Virginius* sprang a leak, or, some say, was scuttled, and found her grave in the ocean depths beneath us.

Recapture of the Emily St. Pierre

The following strange story was told to me many years ago, and, although some of the details have been forgotten, the incident, which was declared to be quite true, led to one of the most extraordinary exploits of the War between the States in the famous recapture of the *Emily St. Pierre.*

While Great Britain was at war with France in the year 1813, a small Scotch brig was approaching the British Channel on the last leg of her voyage from the West Indies for Greenock on the river Clyde. She had successfully eluded strange sails and the captain was quite hopeful of reaching his destination without encountering a French privateer, but alas, when the brig was within a few days' sail of the "land o'cakes," a smarter vessel, bearing the tricolor at her peak, overhauled the Scotsman, and, with a round shot across her bows, compelled her surrender. A French prize crew was placed on board with orders to sail the brig to the nearest French port for adjudication. The Scotch captain and his cabin boy were retained on board as prisoners, the former to assist in the working of the brig and the latter to wait upon the prize crew. With the enemy's flag apeak, the little brig was headed for the enemy's country and was soon alone upon the sea. With the accustomed discipline of the man-of-war somewhat relaxed, the Frenchmen, wishing to make merry over their good fortune, sought among the brig stores the red wine to which they were accustomed, instead of which they broached a cask of Jamaica rum, under whose masterful potency they became as dead men. The Scotsman was quick to seize his opportunity, and with the lone assistance of his cabin boy he dragged every man Jack into his forecastle and securely tied them to their bunks; the officers were likewise secured in the cabin and the course of the brig laid straight and true again for bonnie Scotland. On the following morning while the brig was slowly proceeding under light canvas, which the master himself had set while the boy steered, another Frenchman gave chase and the hopes of the Scotsman gave way to despair as the swift cruiser overhauled him hand over hand. Turning to the French officer whom he had secured to the poop deck for the fresh air, he was astonished to find him in a state of terror instead of in triumph at the prospect of his release. Quickly the Frenchman explained in his own language, with which the Scotch captain was familiar, that his disgraceful plight and that of his crew would result in his speedy

Captain William Wilson.

courtmartial and execution at the yard arm; that if the Scotch captain would accept his parole, restore to him his uniform and sword, assume with his cabin boy the uniforms of two of his Frenchmen, hoist the French ensign and leave the rest to him, he would extricate the brig, resume his bonds, and cast his lot in Scotland, for he could never see his own country again. This was quickly done, for the alternative but assured the brig's recapture. On came the armed Frenchman. Boom! went one of her guns. The brig rounded to, and in response to his countryman's hail, the quondam prize master

The **Emily St. Pierre** *under sail.*

shouted through his trumpet that he was of the French privateer, in charge of a prize ship, taking her to a French port. The commander of the armed vessel waved a salute and sailed away quite satisfied. The *status quo ante* of the brig was resumed, as arranged, the Clyde was reached in safety, and the descendants of the French prize crew can account for some of the mysterious French names still heard in the Scottish Highlands to this day. And, *mirabile dictu*, the cabin boy of the brig became the hero of the following true story and was subsequently well known as the captain of Confederate blockade-running steamer into Wilmington. It was during the fourth year of the war that this very extraordinary man, Capt. William Wilson, appeared in Cape Fear waters in command of a steamer which ran the blockade at Wilmington perhaps three or four times; but there was nothing unusual about this incident, and perhaps for that reason I have forgotten her name. There was, however, something very unusual about Wilson, whose unequalled bravery in recapturing his ship the *Emily St. Pierre*, of Charleston, S.C., in 1861, was, of all the stirring incidents of the blockade, the most admirable example of personal pluck and endurance. I have been told by a kinsman of Miss Emily St. Pierre, for whom the ship was named, that she still lives in

Charleston, and I am repeating this story of Wilson's wonderful exploits at his request. Although not strictly a story of the Cape Fear, it will be none the less interesting to our readers, and I reproduce the account published in *Chambers's Edinburg Journal* entitled "A Matter-of-Fact Story."

"On the morning of the 18th of March, 1862, the Liverpool ship *Emily St. Pierre* (William Wilson, captain) arrived within about twelve miles of Charleston and signaled for a pilot. She had made a long and tedious voyage of four months from Calcutta, bound for St. John, New Brunswick, calling at Charleston for orders if Charleston was open. If the Southern port was blockaded, Captain Wilson's orders were to proceed direct to the British port of St. John, New Brunswick. The ship had formerly belonged to Charleston, but since the outbreak of the American Civil War she had sailed under the English flag. Her nominal owners were Messrs. Fraser, Trenholm & Co., of 10 Rumford Place, Liverpool, a firm doing an extensive business, who had very close relations with the Confederate or Southern States, for whom they acted as bankers and agents in this country.

"Upon approaching the Charleston Bar, the ship was hailed by a vessel which proved to be the Northern cruiser *James Adger*, and in response Captain Wilson hauled up his courses, backed his main yard, and lay to. An American naval lieutenant and a score of men came on board and demanded his papers. The manifest showed an innocent cargo, 2,000 bales of gunny bags, and the registration of the ship as English was in due order. Charleston being blockaded, the captain demanded permission to proceed to his destination, the British port of St. John. The lieutenant refused, and referred the matter to his superior in command; and the two vessels proceeded into Charleston roadstead, where they arrived at half past two in the afternoon.

"Captain Wilson was ordered on board the flagship of the blockading squadron, the *Florida*, where he was kept for two hours in solitude and suspense. At last a flag officer, Captain Goldsboro, came to him and said they had decided to seize the *Emily St. Pierre* on several grounds. He asserted that she carried contraband of war—namely, saltpeter; that her English registration was not bona fide; that many articles on board had been found bearing the name Charleston; that the same word had been scraped out on her stern and the name Liverpool substituted; that Captain Wilson had not disclosed all his papers, but had been observed from the *James Adger* to throw overboard and sink a small parcel, probably of incriminating documents. Captain Wilson protested and appealed to the maritime law of nations, but in vain. He was informed that the law courts of Philadelphia would adjudicate the matter; and finally Captain Wilson was invited to take passage in his vessel to Philadelphia and to place at the disposal of the navigator his charts and instruments. The invitation in form was in fact a command. He returned to his vessel to find that his crew had all been removed, with the exception of two who were not sailors—the steward, named Matthew Montgomery, and the cook, named Louis Schevlin, hailing from Frankfort-on-the-Main. These were merely passengers and with them was an American engineer who had obtained permission to take passage to Philadelphia.

"The prize crew who took charge of the vessel consisted of Lieutenant Stone, of the United States Navy, in command; a master's mate and twelve men, fourteen in all; with the American passenger, fifteen. The moment that Captain Wilson again stepped aboard his own vessel, he formed the resolution to recapture her and take her home. He was bold enough to think that it might be possible to recapture the ship even against such odds. An unarmed man, aided by the questionable support of a steward and a cook, was practically powerless against the fifteen of the crew. On the other hand, Captain Wilson was a brawny, big-framed Scotsman (a native of Dumfriesshire), a thorough seaman, determined in resolve, cool and prompt in action. He called the steward and the cook to him in his stateroom and disclosed the wild project he had formed. Both manfully promised to stand by their chief. This was at half past four on the morning of the 21st of March, the third day out from Charleston. Captain Wilson had already formed his plan of operations, and had prepared to a certain extent for carrying it out. With the promise of the cook and the steward secured, he lost no time, gave them no chance for their courage to evaporate, but proceeded at once in the darkness and silence of the night to carry out his desperate undertaking. He was prepared to lose his life or to have his ship; that was the simple alternative.

"It was Lieutenant Stone's watch on deck, and the prize master's mate was asleep in his berth. The Scotch captain went into the berth, handed out the mate's sword and revolvers, clapped a gag made of a piece of wood and some marline between his teeth, seized his hands, which Montgomery, the steward, quickly ironed, and so left him secure. The lieutenant still paced the deck, undisturbed by a sound. Then across to another stateroom, where the American engineer lay asleep. He also was gagged and ironed silently and without disturbance. His revolvers and those already secured were given to the steward and the cook, who remained below in the cabin. Captain Wilson went on deck.

"Lieutenant Stone was pacing the deck, and the watch consisted of one man at the helm, one at the lookout, on the forecastle, and three others who were about the ship. For ten minutes Captain Wilson walked up and down, remarking on the fair wind, and making believe that he had just turned out. The ship was off Cape Hatteras, midway of their journey between Charleston and Philadelphia, the most easterly projection of the land on that coast. It is difficult navigation thereabouts, with the cross currents and a tendency to fogs, affording the two captains subject for talk.

" 'Let her go free a bit, Captain Stone; you are too close to the cape. I tell you and I know.'

" 'We have plenty of offing,' replied the lieutenant; and then to the helmsman: 'How's her head?'

" 'Northeast and by east, sir,' came the reply.

" 'Keep her so. I tell you it is right,' said the lieutenant.

" 'Well, of course I am not responsible now, but I am an older sailor than you, Captain Stone, and I tell you if you want to clear Hatteras, another two points east will do no harm. Do but look at my chart; I left it open on the cabin table. And the coffee will be ready now,' and Captain Wilson led the way from the poop to the cabin, followed by the commander.

"There was a passage about five yards long leading from the deck to the cabin, a door at either end. The captain stopped at the first door, closing it, and picking from behind it an iron belaying pin which he had placed there. The younger man went forward to the cabin where the chart lay upon the table.

" 'Stone!' The lieutenant turned at the sudden peremptory exclamation of his name. His arm upraised, the heavy iron bolt in his hand, in low, but hard, eager, quick words, 'My ship shall never go to Philadelphia!' said the captain. He did not strike. It was unnecessary. Montgomery had thrust the gag in the young lieutenant's mouth; he was bound hand and foot, bundled into a berth, and the door locked. Three out of fifteen were thus disposed of. There was still the watch on deck and the watch below.

"The construction of the *Emily St. Pierre* was of a kind not unusual, but still not very common. The quarters of the crew were not in the forecastle, but in a roundhouse amidships. The name does not describe its shape. It was an oblong house on deck with windows and one door. From the poop, or upper deck, at the stern, over the cabins and staterooms and the passage before mentioned, there was a companion stair on the port side leading to the deck at the waist; whilst a similar companionway at the stern led down to the level of the deck, which could also be approached direct from the cabins through the passage. In this space, behind the poop, was the wheel, slightly raised, for the steersman to see clear of the poop; and there was a hatchway leading to the lazaret hold, a small supplementary hold usually devoted to stores, extra gear, coils of spare rope, and so on. Nothing that might be done on this part of the deck could be seen, therefore, from the waist of the ship; vice versa, except by the steersman, who was elevated by a step or two above the level.

"Coming on this part of the deck from the cabin, Captain Wilson called to the three men who were about, and pointing to a heavy coil of rope in the lazaret, ordered them to get it up at once—Lieutenant Stone's orders. They jumped down without demur, suspecting nothing, as soon as the captain shoved the hatch aside. They were no sooner in than he quickly replaced and fastened the hatch. The three were securely trapped in full view of the helmsman, whose sailor's instinct kept him in his place at the wheel.

" 'If you utter a sound or make a move,' said the captain, showing a revolver, 'I'll blow your brains out!' and then he called aft the lookout man, the last of the watch on deck. The man came aft. Would he help to navigate the ship to England? No; he would not. He was an American. Then would he call the watch? He would do that. And eagerly he did it; but the next moment he was laid low on the deck, and bundled unceremoniously into the lazaret with his three companions, the hatchway replaced and secured, Captain Wilson standing on guard near by.

"Meanwhile the watch below had been called and were astir. When sailors tumble out they generally do so gradually and by twos and threes. The first two that came aft were quickly overpowered, one at a time, and bound. The third man drew his knife and dashed at the steward, who fired, wounding him severely in the shoulder. It was the only shot that was fired. Finding that cook and steward and captain were all armed, the rest of the watch below quietly surrendered, and submitted to be locked in the roundhouse, prisoners of the bold and resolute man who in the course of an hour had thus regained possession of his ship against overwhelming odds.

"For England! Yes, homeward bound in an unseaworthy ship; for a ship that is undermanned is unseaworthy to the last degree. It is worse than overloading. And here is our brave captain 3,000 miles from home calmly altering her course the few points eastward he had recommended to the lieutenant, homeward bound for England, his crew a steward and a cook! Neither could steer, nor hand, nor reef. Brave-hearted Matthew Montgomery, honest Louis Schevlin, now is the time to show what savor of seamanship you have picked up amongst your pots and pans of the galley and the pantry.

"The first thing was to wash and bandage the wounded shoulder of the man who was shot, the next to put all the prisoners in the roundhouse under lock and key. Four of them out of twelve volunteered to assist in working the ship rather than submit to the tedium of imprisonment. The irony of fate. But one of the four could steer, and he imperfectly. And the courses are set, and the topsails, lower and upper, are drawing and the topgallant sails, too—pray Heaven this wind may last and no stronger.

"The lieutenant was admitted to the captain's table under guard and on parole. The meal over, he was ushered into his stateroom and locked in. Once a day only—for the captain is captain and crew combined—bread and beef and water were passed to the prisoners in the roundhouse; no more attention than absolutely necessary could be spared to them.

"Homeward bound! Captain Wilson had overcome his captors; could he overcome the elements? The glass was falling, the wind was rising, threatening a gale. The reef tackles were passed to the capstan, so that one man's strength could haul them. Then the wheel was resigned to the Irish steward and German cook, whilst the captain had to lie aloft and tie the reef points, ever and anon casting a look behind and signaling to his faithful men how to move the wheel. Hours of hard work, fearful anxiety before all is made snug to meet the fury of the coming storm. All is right at last, thought the captain, if everything holds.

"Yes, if. Everything did not hold. The tiller was carried away in the midst of the gale, and Captain Wilson, brave heart as he was, felt the sadness of despair. He had been keeping watch day and night without intermission for many days, snatching an hour's sleep at intervals, torn with anxiety, wearied with work. It was but a passing faintness of the heart. The ship rolled and tossed, helmless, at the mercy of the sea. For twelve hours he wrought to rig up a jury rudder, and at last, lifting up his heart in gratitude, for the second time he snatched his ship out of the hands of destruction; for the second time he could inform Lieutenant Stone that he was in command of his own ship. No longer was the ship buffetted at the mercy of the wild wind and the cruel Atlantic rollers, but her course was laid true and her head straight—for England.

"For thirty days they sailed with westerly gales behind them. They made the land in safety, and the code signal was hoisted as they passed up the English Channel. On the morning of the 21st of April, exactly one month since her course was altered on Cape Hatteras, the *Emily St. Pierre* threaded the devious channels which led into the broad estuary of the Mersey, the anchor fell with a plunge and an eager rattle of the leaping cable, and the ship rode stately on the rushing tide.

"Much was made of Captain Wilson during the next few weeks. All England rang with applause of his brave exploit. Meetings were convened, presentations were made, speeches were delivered to the extent that might have turned the head of a less simple and true-hearted man. Large sums of money were subscribed, of which plucky Matthew Montgomery and honest Louis Schevlin, the cook, got their share. But probably the happiest and proudest moment of his life was when the captain stood on deck on the day of the arrival, his wife by his side, near her the owner of the ship, Charles K. Prioleau, of Fraser, Trenholm & Co., whilst he narrated in simple words the story of his exploit. His big beard was torn and ragged, his eyes blood-shot with weariness and loss of sleep, his face haggard, weather-beaten, and drawn; but he was a man of whom all Britain was proud, a man to inspire her with the faith that the race of heroes does not die."

The Lilians Last Successful Run

The four years of blockade running, from 1861 to 1865, were so crowded with incidents and adventures of an extraordinary and startling nature that each day brought a new and novel experience.

I recall my first day under fire, the trembling knees, the terrifying scream of the approaching shells, the dread of instant death. Again, the notable storm at sea in which our ship was buffetted and lashed by the waves until the straining steel plates cut the rivets and the fireroom was flooded and the engines stopped, while the tempest tossed us helpless upon the mountainous waves and all hope of our lives was gone, until we were mercifully cast upon a reef which extends about thirty miles from Bermuda. Again, when our party of five persons, endeavoring to reach the Confederacy in a small launch after the fall of Fort Fisher, was cast away the second day upon Green Turtle Cay, an obscure island of the Bahamas, where we dwelt in a negro's hut for three weeks, and then foolishly risked our lives again for two weeks at sea in a small boat which landed us in the surf among the man-eating sharks off Cape Canaveral, in Florida.

In the narration of these reminiscences of war times on the Cape Fear, I have adhered to facts, supported, when in doubt, by official records. In the following story of my personal adventures, I have written some extraordinary incidents which came under my observation, although not in the sequence described; and the romantic features are based on a true incident of the war, the hero of which, Captain M——, still lives in an honored old age. For uniformity, I have changed the text as it appeared in the *Charlotte Observer* many years ago, by the substitution of real names.

Abstract Log of *U.S.S. Shenandoah.*
"Saturday, July 30, 1864. At meridian, latitude (D.R.) 33 50 N.; longitude (D.R.) 76 16 W., latitude (observed) 34 01 N., longitude (by chronometer) 76 10 W. At 3.45 p.m. sighted a steamer burning black smoke to the eastward; made all sail in chase. At 4.30 p.m. made stranger out to be a double smokestack, side-wheel steamer, apparently a blockade runner, standing to the northward and westward. At 5.45 he showed rebel colors. Called the first division and powder division to quarters and began to fire at her with the 30 and 150 pounder rifle Parrott. At 6 p.m. beat to quarters and fired all the divisions. At 7 p.m. took in fore-topgallant sail and foresail. At 7.30 took in fore-topsail. During the chase fired 70 rounds from 30-pounder Parrott, 18 rounds from 11-inch guns, and one round from 24-pounder howitzer. At 8 p.m. stopped firing, gave up the chase, stopped engines. At 9.20 Cape Lookout Light bore N. E. by N., 14 miles distant. Sounded in 12 fathoms of water. First saw the steamer in latitude 33 34, N., longitude 76 33 W. At midnight Cape Lookout Light bore N.E. by N. 1/2 N., distant seventeen miles.

"(Signed) Acting Master,
U.S. Navy."

This matter-of-fact entry, read at random from the official records of the war, stirs my blood, because I, then seventeen years of age, was purser of that blockade runner, and it was I who hoisted those "rebel" colors on that eventful day fifty-five years ago; and thereby hangs a tale.
The steamer *Lilian* was one of the most successful examples of a Clyde-built blockade runner of 1864 in design and equipment. Of 500 tons net register, with two rakish funnels, the finest marine oscillating engines, a battery of boilers which drove her fifteen knots an hour, and loaded to her

The **C.S.S. Albemarle** *after her capture by Lt. William B. Cushing.*

marks, she presented to the critical eye the graceful appearance of a racing yacht. A thing of beauty and a joy forever she was to all of us on board, and our beloved chief, the celebrated John Newland Maffitt, no less, was, we thought, the man of all men to command her. Unluckily for us he was ordered to take charge of the ram *Albemarle*, which the intrepid Cushing later destroyed—the most conspicuous example of personal daring recorded in the history of the war.

Another Southern man succeeded him, and, we having received from the Confederate agent a cargo of mysterious packages, which was most carefully handled, proceeded from St. George, Bermuda, bound for the port of Wilmington, N.C. This desired haven of these fugitives of the sea was preferred to the more difficult blockaded ports farther south. There were two inlets, Main Bar or Western Channel, commanded by Fort Caswell, and New Inlet, guarded by that Malakoff of the South, Fort Fisher.

Many fine ships were lost in sight of these defenses when daylight overtook a belated landfall, and it was pitiful to watch the desperate efforts of the little greyhounds to run the gauntlet of the fleet, whose concentrated fire at close range sometimes drove them among the breakers, where many wrecks may still be seen after all these years. There were many more fortunate, whose daring roused to the highest pitch of enthusiasm the brave fellows of the Confederate garrison who manned the protecting guns which kept the fleet at a respectful distance.

As we passed the ships which lined the docks of the friendly islands of Bermuda, their crews were mustered and cheer after cheer greeted us from lusty throats in unison. Beyond the bar we sailed upon a tranquil sea, without a sail in sight, and then I paid each man his bounty of $40 gold, an earnest of the greater sum which he would get for a successful run.

Upon our ship the discipline was rigorous and unrelenting. To each was given in few words his orders for the run; sobriety, silence, and civility were enforced. Our Chief Engineer Lockhart, Chief Officer Vogel, Pilot Jim Billy Craig, our Signal Officer Fred Gregory and I were served at the captain's table; the other officers messed together. Our crew numbered 48 men.

When night drew on the finest Welsh coal was picked and piled upon the boiler-room plates, for use in an emergency, and the dexterous handling of the dampers prevented the telltale sparks from betraying our dangerous course across the line of the ever-watchful cruisers, which formed their cordon around the Bermudas, upon the edge of the Gulf Stream, and across the most dangerous approaches to the Cape Fear River. No lights were permitted, smoking was inhibited, as, through impenetrable darkness, we ran full speed for Dixie's land.

A double watch was kept aloft, and upon the turtleback well forward, and the keenest eyes were fixed upon the course to guard against a collision with watchful cruisers, which also masked their lights.

Next in importance to the Wilmington pilot, Jim Billy Craig, who was a man of great ability, was a long thin fellow, a landsman, a nondescript known as "the watchman," who held himself in readiness day and night for service as a special lookout. This person's vision was wonderfully clear and far-reaching. He could see an object on the darkest night quite invisible to the rest of us, and his most efficient service was in the hour before daylight, when proximity to Uncle Sam's gunboats was most undesirable. Several easy captures had been made in the first streak of dawn by the accidental meeting of a casual cruiser and his unhappy quarry, when escape by speed was simply impossible. It was for this reason that our Long Tom was retained at high wages, which he squandered with other prodigals in playing crackaloo with double gold eagles. It was a simple game; two or more persons each threw up a gold piece, the one falling upon a joint or crack in the deck winning the others which fell between the lines. This was forbidden at sea, but such discipline was relaxed in port.

Our first night at sea was clear and beautiful, the air, cool and grateful, contrasted with the severe and at times almost suffocating warmth of the limestone islands. After the evening meal, Gregory and I, snugly ensconced in the lee of the cabin, which was on deck, sat far into the night gazing with wonder upon the tranquil glory of the stars, which shone with exceeding splendor, and talking with sad hearts of the waning light of the star of the Confederacy, which had reached its zenith at Chancellorsville and which sank so disastrously at the later battle of Gettysburg. The wind was light, but the rush of the staunch little ship at full speed brought to our listening ears the faint sound of a bell, not that of a ship striking the change of the watch, but a continuous peal of irregular strokes. In a few moments it ceased, and I have often wondered what it meant, for no sail was visible that night. Alert and eager for its repetition, which came not, our wonderment was increased by the cry of a human voice in the darkness ahead, which was also observed by the lookouts aloft and alow, and, while Long Tom was rapidly climbing the ratlines of the foremast to the crosstrees, our captain appeared on the bridge and brought the ship to a full stop. In painful silence all eyes and ears were strained to catch a sight or sound from the mysterious object ahead. Again and again the long-drawn, wailing cry. Could it be a castaway? The sailor's instinct and sympathy is never so much aroused as by such an incident. Shifting our course a point or two, we proceeded slowly ahead; the cry grew clearer, with despairful lamentations; again our course was changed, the paddles slowly turning. Ignoring the usual precaution of silence on board at night, the captain ordered the officer of the deck to answer with a hail. Immediately the voice responded, and in a few moments Long Tom reported to the commander on the bridge, "A nigger in a ship's boat, sir." "What," said the captain, "can he be doing out here in a boat 160 miles from land?" "I'm blessed if I know, sir, but I'm telling you the truth." "Castaway, sir, close aboard," was the second officer's report a few moments later. "Heave him a line," said the commander. The falls of the davits were soon hooked on and the boat, with its lonesome occupant, hoisted to the deck. The next morning, when I was dressing, the chief steward knocked at my door and gravely asked if I would see the man whom we had rescued the night before, "for," said he, "there is something mysterious about his plight which he refuses to make known to me." On going forward I found a negro man of about fifty years of age, apparently in deep distress; mutual recognition was

*The **Lilian** threading her way beween two Union blockaderss.*

instantaneous; the poor fellow fell at my feet and embraced my knees, with broken sobs of "Oh, Marse Jeems, Marse Jeems, Marse Jeems!" His story was soon told in the homely and pathetic vernacular of the old-time Southern darkey. He had long been the butler and body servant of my friend at Orton plantation, whose lovely daughter had given her heart to a manly young neighbor before he went away to the war which had desolated many Southern homes. The fearful news of disaster had come from Gettysburg, in which her lover was engaged with his company on Culp's Hill. He had been shot through the lungs and was left dying on the field, which was later occupied by the enemy. Then a veil was drawn, for all subsequent inquiries as to his death and the disposal of his body were unavailing. The poor girl at Orton, grief stricken, haunted by fears of the worst, and mocked by her efforts to seek him beyond the lines, slowly faded to a shadow of her former self. Again and again my friend returned from a hopeless search among the living and the dead, when, he, too, began to pine away, for the war had robbed him of all but the child whom he adored, and now she was slipping away from him. It was then that this Nature's nobleman in a black skin came forward and desired his liberty to go through the lines in Virginia and never return until he brought the body dead, or news of his young master living, to the dear mistress whom he loved more than his own life. In vain my friend refused. How could he, a slave, overcome obstacles which the master, with all his influence, had failed to overcome? At last he gave the desired pass to proceed to the missing boy's command upon this mission of mercy, which was countersigned by the proper authority, and the faithful fellow proceeded on foot toward his destination. What followed, "in weariness and painfulness, in watchings often, in hunger and thirst, in fastings often, in cold and nakedness," would fill a volume. He reached the regiment at last, and carried to many hungry hearts the news of their loved ones at home, but he was told that his quest was in vain; the captain was dead, a Federal surgeon who approached him on the field had found his wounds mortal, had received from him his sword, to be sent home to the young mistress, with fond words of his devotion to the last; he had better return home. But no, he attempted that night to slip through the lines toward the Federal Army; he was caught, brought back, and sentenced to be shot at sunrise. How he was saved, as by a miracle, through the recognition of the officer of the firing squad, and sent back to Wilmington need not be told.

He had formed another desperate resolve—he would go to Orton in the night, and in a frail bateau attempt to pass the picket boats at Fort Anderson and Fort Fisher, and reach the blockading fleet beyond the bar. Perhaps when they heard his story they would take pity and send him North, when he might resume his search. He had crossed the river by the Market Street ferry and was passing through the cotton yard, where several blockade runners were loading their outward cargoes, when a new idea came to him; why could he not go as a steward on a steamer, and, with his wages, reach the North by way of the West Indies? With deferential humility he approached the captain of a steamer, which shall be nameless. He was not an American, neither was he a man in the sense of the noblest work of God; he was the embodiment of a personal devil; he laughed the old man to scorn; he had carried away on previous voyages runaway niggers, who, he said, had stowed away, and he had been obliged to pay for them on his return; the next one he caught at sea on board his ship would wish he had never been born; he didn't need a steward, and he did not doubt his tale of the young master was a lie. As the poor man turned away he was drawn aside by a kindly steward who had overheard the conversation, and, after much discussion and apprehension, he agreed to arrange a secret passage to Bermuda. That night he was stowed away, where it was hoped that the cruel process of fumigation for the discovery of fugitive slaves and deserters from the army, then in vogue before sailing, would not reach him. Cramped by the narrow space which forbade lying down, and deathly seasick, on the second night he crawled out for fresh air, was detected and seized by a passing sailor and reported to the captain. Infuriated by his recognition of the stowaway, he actually stopped the ship and set the poor wretch adrift in a leaky boat, without oars or food or water. It was on the second night after that he heard the mysterious bell and shrieked aloud for deliverance.

Although these qualities were not a common possession, this remarkable instance of a slave's devotion to his owner was not exceptional.

Captain Charles Manigault Morris.

There were hundreds and perhaps thousands of such examples, especially on the part of those whose duties were of a domestic nature. It was not the evolution of gentle traits of character, for this man's grandfather had lived and died a savage in the wilds of Africa. It was the result of daily contact with refined and kindly people whom he served, whose characteristic urbanity was unconsciously imitated, and whose consideration for others, which constitutes true politeness, was reflected in their servitor's devotion. I have a pensioner at Orton who is ninety-four years of age. He was the personal servant in his youth of Doctor Porcher, of Charleston. He is as polite as a cultivated Frenchman might be, but he is sincere in speech. He uses at times French phrases. He can tell you in polished language, and with becoming deference, of the grand people of the exclusive set of Charleston of long ago, and his solicitude for your health and for that of everyone connected with you whom he has never heard of is shown in expressions of old-time gentility, but he belongs to a class that is passing away.

I have up to this time refrained from mentioning the fact that we had on board, as passengers, three important personages of the old Navy, whose duty, as they saw it, impelled them to resign their commissions in a service which was dear to them, and to cast in their lot for weal or woe with the fortunes of their native State, which had seceded from the Union. They had served with distinction afloat and around the world upon a noted Confederate war vessel, and they were under orders to report to Secretary Mallory at Richmond. At the time of which I write there were in Nassau and in Bermuda certain spies said to have been in the pay of the Federal Government, and they sometimes succeeded in passing themselves, disguised and under assumed names, as sailors and firemen, but more frequently as stewards on the blockade runners that were not careful enough in the selection of their crew. By this means much valuable information was communicated to the authorities at Washington, and the mysterious loss of several fine blockade runners was attributed to the seditious influence of such persons in time of peril. There were also in each of our foreign ports of refuge a few fanatics, who, contrary to the usages of war, and upon their own initiative and responsibility, attempted the destruction of Confederate steamers at sea by secretly hiding in their bunkers imitation lumps of coal, containing explosives of sufficient power to sink a vessel when this object was shoveled into the furnaces under the boilers. Several such attempts had been frustrated because the deception was clumsy and easily detected in time by the coal passers, and I remember that these nefarious undertakings were frequently discussed by the engineers of our ship.

*The **U.S.S. Wachusett** and her commander, Captain Napolean Collins (inset).*

Meanwhile, I observed with some curiosity that we were off our regular course, and also, with feelings of dismay, that we were approaching a long, low, rakish-looking war vessel, barque-rigged and under steam, which was evidently lying to and awaiting us, but my apprehension was changed to wonder and amazement as I beheld flying apeak the new white flag of the Confederacy. It was a sight I shall never forget; alone upon the wide sea, hunted by a hundred adversaries, the corvette *Florida*, under the gallant Maffitt, had circumnavigated the globe and spread consternation among the merchant marine of the Stars and Stripes without the loss of a man. She was a beautiful vessel and had been handled with consummate skill and daring. There was something pathetic in the object of our meeting, which had been secretly prearranged, for a boat was immediately lowered, into which were placed sundry parcels of opium for the hospital service of the Southern Army, probably from the hold of one of her prizes; and this sympathetic offering from these homeless fellows on the high sea to their sick and wounded comrades in the field hospitals, for the mitigation of their sufferings, appealed strongly to our hearts.

We tarried briefly, dipping in a parting salute to each other our respective ensigns, probably the first and the last time that the conquered banner was used to exchange courtesies with the same flag at sea. The corvette proceeded under her new commander, Capt. Charles M. Morris, cruising near and far until she reached Bahia, Brazil, in which neutral port she was attacked while disarmed, and captured at night by the *Wachusett*, and later, it is said, was conveniently cast away near the last resting place of her famous commander, Captain Maffitt.

Our third and last day at sea began auspiciously, but we were drawing toward the coast much farther north than our usual landfall. At about half past three in the afternoon we were startled by the lookout in the crow's nest, with a lusty "Sail ho!" "Whereaway?" called the officer of the watch. "On the port quarter, sir, heading toward us." We were in a bad position, to the northward of Cape Lookout, but the stranger had not yet perceived us. In our eagerness for more steam, however, the telltale smoke was vomited from our funnels, and in a short time it was evident that we were being overhauled by a faster vessel under crowded canvas and full steam. The rising wind favored him, because we had but two sails, fore and aft, which served to steady us in a seaway, but this added little to our speed. As the stranger drew rapidly nearer, pushing us toward a lee shore, she opened fire with her rifled cannon, and for the first time in my life I heard the scream of a hostile shell as it passed between our funnels and plunged into the sea a half mile beyond. The sensation was most unpleasant; had we been able to return the fire, the excitement of battle must have been exhilarating, but to be hunted like a rabbit and pelted with Parrott shells and 11-inch projectiles was enough to reduce my backbone to such laxation that my trembling knees refused to bear it. The cruiser's aim was deadly, for the 11-inch shells came tumbling end over end with such fearful accuracy that many of them passed only a few feet from my head. Others sent the salt spray flying into our faces; and yet there were, up to six o'clock, no casualties of any importance. The admirable conduct of our naval passengers soon inspired me with courage— such is the influence of veterans beside raw troops—and, strangely enough, as the firing of single batteries was changed to broadsides, my despairful feelings gave way to hope and confidence. Our pursuer was now fairly abeam and sailing the same course. Why she did not destroy us utterly at such short range must have appeared to them incomprehensible, because we easily distinguished without glasses the movements of their gunners and the working of their crew at quarters; and our pursuer must have been surprised at the audacity of our passengers, who tranquilly measured with their watches the intervals between the firing of his projectiles and their passage overhead. They also used their sextants continuously during the chase, and it was doubtless owing to their superior knowledge and fortitude that our commander held on his course in the face of imminent destruction, for, be it remembered, we were loaded to the hatch combings with gunpowder for Lee's army. As the sun sank lower on the horizon, so sank our hopes of escape, for every moment seemed to be drawing us nearer to the end. Even our passengers became disheartened and said at last that it was a useless risk to all the lives on board. They accordingly proceeded to their cabins and destroyed their official papers, and threw overboard some valuable side arms and rifles, and I, by the captain's orders, took the Confederate mail bag and government dispatches to the furnace and saw them go up in smoke. Orders were now given to lower the boats to the rail, for what purpose I do not know, when a strange thing happened. There was a loud explosion in the forward fireroom, not made by the bursting of a shell but accompanied by a cloud of steam. Immediately the stokers and firemen swarmed up the iron ladders to the deck, terror-stricken and bewildered. They had been kept at their work for hours at the point of a pistol in the hands of desperate and determined men, but now, panic-stricken, they rushed aft, not knowing what they would do. Our chief engineer quietly reported the collapse of one of our boilers, cause unknown, steam reduced nearly one half in consequence, but our slackened speed proved to be the means of our salvation. The sun had gone behind a cloud bank, a mist hung over the land toeeward, our ship, painted the dull grey color of the sand dunes along the shore line, was obscured from the view of the enemy, which was quite visible to us, forging ahead and firing wildly. Our engines were stopped and sails lowered, every eye was upon the cruiser. Would she discover our desperate expedient? Had she done so, I believe our crew would have been ordered to the boats and the *Lilian* abandoned, with a lighted fuse for her destruction. But the cruiser

Col. John Hedrick, C.S.A.

drew farther away, firing his broadsides at an invisible foe. Cautiously and slowly we limped to windward, crossing the wake of our discomfited antagonist, and laying our course straight and true for Wilmington. It was now eight o'clock in the evening, a hundred miles between us and our dangerous destination, and daylight comes early in the summer months. By the closest calculation we might, without accidents, reach the Cape Fear by sunrise, and then in our disabled condition how could we hope to run the gauntlet of the blockading fleet? It was resolved to do it or die. Fortune had favored us in an extremity, perhaps she would still be kind. We had an anxious night; sleep, even after the excitement and exhaustion of the previous day, was impossible. We saw the first faint streaks of day off Masonboro Sound, where our watchful Gregory picked up the signal lights ashore and passed the word along the beach for our protection by the fort. It was a cloudy morning; on and on we drove the little ship; she seemed to feel the crisis while she labored like a sentient being to meet her fate as speedily as possible. At last, in the friendly haze of dawn, we were among them; blockaders to the right of us, blockaders to the left of us, blockaders ahead of us loomed up like monsters of the deep. Craig coolly but anxiously peered ahead. Long Tom, well forward on the turtleback, whispered the words which a line of picked men reported to the bridge. Again and again we stopped for the passage of a picket barge or gunboat in the darkness ahead, who saw us not, and for the bearings, which in our devious course we had lost in confusion. Once more we slowly proceeded, when suddenly, out of the darkness and close aboard, flashed the fiery train of a rocket, and a deep, commanding voice, just over the side, shouted "Heave to, or I'll sink you." Quickly our bridge responded "Aye, aye, sir, we stop the engines." "Back your engines, sir, and stand by for my boats," called the lusty man-of-war. But our paddles were not reversed. Lockhart said he never heeded such an order with the bar at hand; on the contrary our engines were evidently running away with the ship, and, while the confident blockader, diverted from his guns, was engaged in lowering his boats, the *Lilian* was gliding away toward the bar. A trail of rockets and Drummond lights and bombshells from the rest of the fleet followed in our wake, but the friendly flash of signals from the fort encouraged us, while Gregory, with his masked lights, revealed to them our steady progress until we anchored under the Confederate guns. It was now broad daylight and the blockading fleet had sullenly withdrawn to a safe distance. We proceeded toward Fort Anderson and came to anchor at quarantine. The clouds had passed away, revealing in the brightness of the morning light the stately white columns of Orton House in the distance. Accompanied by our faithful Scipio and escorted beyond the fort by its courteous Colonel Hedrick, we proceeded in silence through St. Philip's churchyard and the dead colonial town of Brunswick, past Russellboro, where Governor Tryon met the first armed colonists (the cradle of American independence), through the long avenue of oaks, where, looking ahead, we beheld a sight which cheered our hearts; my friend and his daughter surrounded by the yelping hounds returning from a chase, for reynard's brush was at her saddlebow. With mutual exclamations of astonishment and delight we learned that the young captain had written by a flag of truce of his convalescence in a Northern hospital. I will not say the touching words that Scipio heard, as, with hands clasped by master and mistress, and with bowed head, he received their tearful benedictions. My friend has long since gone to his eternal rest and Scipio's white soul soon followed him. They are buried at Orton in a grove where the mocking bird builds its nest and sings; where, above the murmur of the tree tops, which bend to the soft south wind, is heard the distant booming of the sea, and in their death they were not divided.

Index

*Stranded blockade runners are indexed in this book as derelict blockade runners.

THE indispensable book of Cape Fear history!

James Sprunt

Chronicles
of the
Cape Fear River
1660 - 1916

There was a time when the Cape Fear was North Carolina's frontier. The Cape Fear has seen pirates and Indian wars, redcoats and patriot militias, and at least two civil wars. It has sired heroes and villains, statesmen and scholars. Among them was James Sprunt, who as a young man braved the Union blockade as purser aboard a sleek blockade runner. In later life Sprunt became a wealthy businessman whose cotton exporting business was at one time the largest in the world. He owned the storied Orton Plantation, overlooking the river that played such a central role in his life. A philanthropist with a love of the Cape Fear as deep as his very bones, James Sprunt also became widely recognized as one of North Carolina's most respected historians. In what many consider to be the crowning achievement of a distinguished career, *Chronicles of The Cape Fear River: 1667-1916* is the monumental history of southeastern North Carolina that is the starting point for all research into the Cape Fear's varied and colorful past. It is the one book that any true lover of Cape Fear history absolutely must have on their bookshelves, and that all historical researchers should turn to when exploring what came before us, here where the river meets the sea.

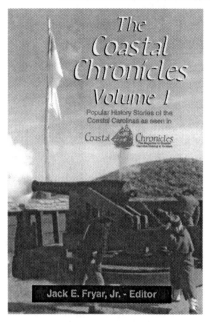
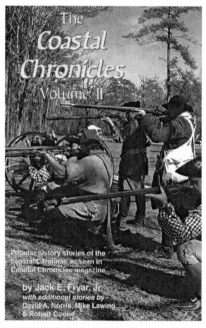

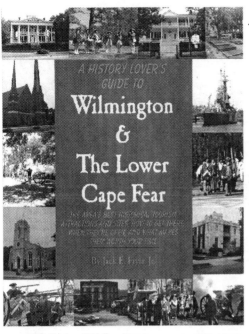
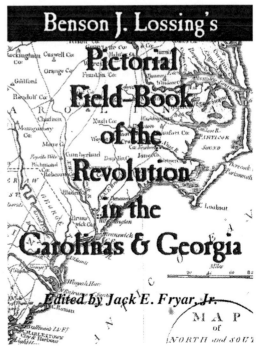

By Beverly Tetterton

Wilmington: *Lost But Not Forgotten*

by Beverly Tetterton

(ISBN 0-9723240-3-8 •
$24.95 • 214 pgs
• Trim Size 8 1/2 x 11 glossy
• Trade Paperback
• Illustrated in Color / B&W)

Beverly Tetterton

With hundreds of rare pictures, *Wilmington: Lost But Not Forgotten* captures the many architectural gems that North Carolina's Port City has lost from the colonial period to the present day. Some were lost to natural disasters like fires and hurricanes. Others fell victim to the "progress" of Urban Renewal or the sometimes short-sightedness of private developers. Regardless of how or why these buildings were torn down and lost, they represent pages ripped from the community's collective history. Preservationist Beverly Tetterton has assembled a collection of lost places that serve as cautionary tales for modern planners and citizens. As we move into the future, preserving the unique character of Wilmington's past is a lesson worth learning.

A superb book for historic preservationists, or for anyone who holds fond memories of the charming place Wilmington and its beaches used to be...

> "*Rebel Gibraltar* surveys the rich history of North Carolina's Cape Fear region in the Civil War, and does so in fascinating detail. It's a dramatic story of a vitally important chapter in the history of the war, and it's well worth any reader's time."
> - Rod Gragg, author of *Confederate Goliath*

James L. Walker, Jr.

REBEL GIBRALTAR

Fort Fisher and Wilmington, C.S.A.

The complete story of the Confederacy's most important port and the forts that defended it throughout the entire Civil War.

With a Forward by Daniel Barefoot, author of *General Robert F. Hoke: Lee's Modest Warrior*

Rebel Gibraltar:
Fort Fisher and Wilmington, C.S.A.
by James L. Walker, Jr.

(ISBN 0-9723240-7-0 • $32.00 • 432 pgs • Trim Size 8 1/2 x 5 1/2 • Trade Paperback • Illustrated)

Called the "Gibraltar of the South," Fort Fisher was the huge earthen fortification that was the linchpin of the Cape Fear defense system in the Civil War. While other books have done excellent jobs of telling the story of the capture of Fort Fisher and Wilmington, James L. Walker, Jr.'s book is the first to cover the fort and the city it protected over the course of the entire war. Copiously illustrated with period photographs and maps by noted mapmaker Mark A. Moore, this is the story of the men in gray who slugged it out on the Cape Fear beaches to protect the lifeblood of the Confederacy coming in on swift and daring blockade runners, and their ultimate defeat in 1865.

James L. Walker, Jr.

Printed in the United States
62228LVS00002B/268-444